The Arts of Literary Criticism

Books by Cat Ellington

REVIEWS BY CAT ELLINGTON: THE COMPLETE ANTHOLOGY, VOL. 1

REVIEWS BY CAT ELLINGTON: THE COMPLETE ANTHOLOGY, VOL. 2

THE MAKING OF DUAL MANIA: FILMMAKING CHICAGO STYLE

REVIEWS BY CAT ELLINGTON – THE COMPLETE ANTHOLOGY LIMITED EDITION HOLIDAY GIFT SET (BOOKS 1 & 2)

REVIEWS BY CAT ELLINGTON: THE COMPLETE ANTHOLOGY, VOL. 3

MORE IMAGINATIVE THAN ORDINARY SPEECH: THE POETRY OF CAT ELLINGTON

REVIEWS BY CAT ELLINGTON: A TRILOGY OF UNIQUE CRITIQUES #1

MEMOIRS IN GOGYOHKA: A BOOK OF SHORT POEMS AND MEMOIRS

YOU CAN QUOTE ME ON THAT: A COLLECTION OF QUOTES BY CAT ELLINGTON

REVIEWS BY CAT ELLINGTON: THE COMPLETE ANTHOLOGY, VOL. 4

REVIEWS BY CAT ELLINGTON: THE COMPLETE ANTHOLOGY, VOL. 5

REVIEWS BY CAT ELLINGTON: THE COMPLETE ANTHOLOGY, VOL. 6

I DO: SHEET MUSIC

THE BOOK OF US: SHEET MUSIC

I'M STILL IN LOVE: SHEET MUSIC

SOMETHING IN YOUR EYES: SHEET MUSIC

GETT OUT: SHEET MUSIC

THE FIVE-STAR REVIEW: A COLLECTION OF CAT ELLINGTON'S TOP-RATED BOOK REVIEWS FROM 1981-2021

STRIKE A PROSE: A FRAMEWORK OF MEMORIES AND COMMENTARIES IN POETRY

REVIEWS BY CAT ELLINGTON: A TRILOGY OF UNIQUE CRITIQUES #2

REVIEWS BY CAT ELLINGTON: THE COMPLETE ANTHOLOGY, VOL. 7

REVIEWS BY CAT ELLINGTON: THE COMPLETE ANTHOLOGY, VOL. 8

REVIEWS BY CAT ELLINGTON: THE COMPLETE ANTHOLOGY, VOL. 9

REVIEWS BY CAT ELLINGTON: A TRILOGY OF UNIQUE CRITIQUES #3

DUAL MANIA (MUSIC FROM THE ORIGINAL SOUNDTRACK ALBUM) PIANO/GUITAR/CHORDS - SHEET MUSIC BOOK

THE COMPLETE WORKS: REVIEWS BY CAT ELLINGTON, BOOKS 1-9

THE ARTS OF LITERARY CRITICISM: THRILLERS IN TANKA, BOOK 1

The Arts of Literary Criticism
Thrillers in Tanka, Book 1

Cat Ellington

Quill Pen Ink Publishing
THE BEAUTY OF EXPRESSION™
CHICAGO

The Arts of Literary Criticism: Thrillers in Tanka, Book 1
Copyright ©2025 Cat Ellington

PAPERBACK EDITION ISBN: 979-8-9918739-0-1

HARDCOVER EDITION ISBN: 979-8-9918739-1-8

DIGITAL EDITION ISBN: 979-8-9918739-2-5

Library of Congress Control Number: 2024951517

All rights reserved. No part of this publication may be reproduced or transmitted in any form or by any means electronic, including photocopy, recording, or any information storage and retrieval system, without permission in writing from the copyright owner.

Cover illustration design: Victoria Rusyn
The Arts' cover Hue: Lilac Shimmer
The Cat Ellington™ Literary Collection
The Cat Ellington™ Poetry Collection

Crows in Watercolor by Digital Art for Digitalartfulworld appear courtesy of Quill Pen Ink Publishing

Published by Quill Pen Ink Publishing
Chicago, Illinois, USA

Quill Pen Ink Publishing, 2025

Printed in the U.S.A.

Table of Contents

Dedication

Preface

Foreword

Chapter 1: **(P)** Unveiling Merciless Women

"The Great Proverbs"

"Misled by Folly"

Chapter 2: **(O)** Hunting Serial Killers

"Ruination"

"Death and Decay"

Chapter 3: **(E)** Analyzing the Wicked Nature of Man

"Blind Spots"

"The Dawn of AI"

Chapter 4: **(T)** Exposing the Lie of Falsehood

"The Way of Death"

"The Dirty River ~~Seine~~ Sin"

Chapter 5: **(R)** Unmasking Deformed Faces

"The Monsters Are Due on Alton Road"

"The Ultimate Finality"

Chapter 6: **(Y)** Hoodwinking and False Impressions

"Metaphor"

"A ~~Tale~~ Tell of Delusions"

Acknowledgments

Coming Soon: The Arts of Literary Criticism: Romance in Haiku, Book 2

About the Author

Dedication

To the memory of the great Rod Serling—
One of my most beloved writing influences

Preface

Dear reader,

If you're reading these words, you are about to witness my latest creative vision: *The Arts of Literary Criticism: Thrillers in Tanka, Book 1*—the first release in The Arts series, featuring crows in watercolor.

While wrapping up my first literary series, Reviews by Cat Ellington, I fell into meditation mode, enjoying the wisdom of a spiritual mind. And, as usual, I was grabbing as much understanding as I could absorb. As many of you know—those of you who are familiar with my style of literary criticism—when I compose my reviews, I build my critiques on spiritual foundations so that my readers will gain a deeper understanding of the wiles of spiritual warfare in the human mind that eventually result in the many afflictions and chaos we witness in the real world daily: cause and effect. It is always wise to start within because it is there where you will find all the answers. If you understand the spiritual aspects, dear reader, you will understand the human condition. It is more important to know the goings-on spiritually than the perception of the surface. Because the surface, the flesh, is deceptive. But once you understand the spiritual, you will find it easier to dissect the physical: this, dear reader, is my traditional method of critiquing fictional characters—who are only a reflection of reality—which, by the way, brings me back to the subject of the latest work in my bibliography, centered on my profession as a literary critic: my new book series, The Arts.

For The Arts series, I imagined paying tribute to a variety of my favorite literary genres and then selecting (watercolor) painted birds that represented the spiritual nature of each genre and the spiritual nature of the characters portrayed in the books; for Thrillers, the black crow is the featured bird. I also envisioned adding works of poetry to each book in the new series that would coincide with every title under review in its respective issue. For me, it would be a project that I could not WAIT to get started on. My right hand was "itching" to write the works of poetry for the series, and I desired to bring in micropoetry. I chose the Japanese genre of Tanka (pronounced Täŋ-kə) to lead the way for the first book in The Arts series, Thrillers, and to set the tone for its soon-to-be-published predecessors. The three art forms of painting, poetry, and literary criticism combine to establish my take on The Arts.

Dear reader, this is my passion; it has been since childhood. And I am honored—and beyond excited—to get this latest series, a body of work in the making for nearly four years, underway. I've posted about it on my social media channels since last year, and it is finally here. On behalf of Quill Pen Ink Publishing, dear reader, I present *The Arts of Literary Criticism: Thrillers in Tanka, Book 1*.

Do enjoy! ;)

Introduction

My dearest reader,

Welcome to the new era of my career in literary criticism! With my cherished Reviews by Cat Ellington series (the one that started it all) in the rearview, I am moving forward with my latest series, The Arts, which will put a new twist on my work as a literary critic. As I visualized how to create The Arts series, excitement boiled in me when I began to get the visions of adding paintings and poetry as borders for my analyses. These three art forms combine to represent the creative arts, my passion.

When the creative juices started to flow, I went berserk with the ideas that were entering my mind; I was in the zone, hyperventilating with glee and enthusiasm. I couldn't WAIT to start putting it all together! I imagined what to do and how to do it; it had to suit me. It had to be unique and distinctive. The Arts series would have to be stylish, you know? The new series that symbolizes my love of reading and composing analyses would have to include two of the things I love most in the creative arts: poetry writing and painted art.

And so it would.

Guided by the Spirit, I searched the cover art I would use for the series, selecting the single illustration of the talented Victoria Rusyn and dubbing its color hue: Lilac Shimmer. Next, I pondered what style of poetry would be suitable for the new series. Here, the vision entailed short poetry, and I couldn't agree more. Micropoetry would be it. I love it! I love the art form. If you all recall, I also composed micropoetry pieces for *More Imaginative Than Ordinary Speech* and *Memoirs in Gogyohka*. But for The Arts series, each book would feature an individual genre of micropoetry to help elaborate the storylines of the books I review in the issues.

Now for the paintings. The vision I received was of birds—various species of birds. Every book in the series will feature individual literary genres and birds – the latter being a symbolic representation of the spiritual aspects of each genre. For Thrillers, book one in The Arts series, I selected the black crow to represent the dark and suspenseful undertones of the thriller genre. Following the vision I received for this series, I had to have the crows in watercolor. I am enthralled, for lack of a better word, with watercolor paints, and I knew it would be a fun process to search for the perfect paintings of black crows. I soon found what I was looking for, and on the pages of Thrillers, an array of large crows, painted perched, precede each critique.

Speaking of fun, I must get back to the poetry contribution. Once I decided that the micropoetry genre of Tanka (pronounced Täŋ-kə)—a classical Japanese form of poetry, respectively—would be the style used to complement the thriller genre in this issue, I went full steam ahead in readiness to start composing the short pieces, five lines, thirty-one syllables each. My job was to create a Tanka for every review present in this issue. Twelve in total. And I had a ball doing it. God, I was going crazy in the creative process, my dear reader. It was crazy fun, FUN! (Laughs) And then I decided to do something else that I thought was (really) exciting. Because poetry is a six-letter word, and there are six chapters in this issue (book one), I created a structure of freestyle poetry to complement the chapters and end in one single work. The first letter of every sentence in the structure spells the word P-O-E-T-R-Y. This idea, by the way, was inspired by the Book of Ecclesiastes. The freestyle poem represents the titles under my critique in this issue, including *One of the Girls* (Lucy Clarke), *The New One* (Evie Green), *Symphony of Secrets* (Brendan Slocumb), *Gone Tonight* (Sarah Pekkanen), *What The Neighbors Saw* (Melissa Adelman), and *The Influencer* (Miranda Rijks), among others.

The works of Tanka on these pages coincide with each book under review and include "*The Great Proverbs*," "*The Dawn of AI*," "*The Way of Death*," "*The Dirty River ~~Seine~~ Sin*," "*A ~~Tale~~ Tell of Delusions*," and many more.

My dear reader, I welcome you to the first release from my new series, *The Arts of Literary Criticism, Thrillers in Tanka, Book 1*, which, I should proudly add, is graced with a foreword written by my fellow writer and Chicago theater critic B.J. Patterson.

I sincerely hope, my dear reader, that you will enjoy not only this first title in my all-new The Arts series but every succeeding title until the progression is complete. Now, without further ado, dear reader? Shall we get on with it? Indeed, we shall. Thank you for viewing.

Foreword

When I first met Cat Ellington in 1993, we were working on the book *The Making of Dual Mania: Filmmaking Chicago Style* (originally titled *Guerilla Filmmaking – Chicago Style),* the blow-by-blow daily diary of the making of the Indie-award-winning film written, produced, and directed by her husband, filmmaker Joseph Strickland. Then, as now, I was utterly blown away by the scope of her capacity to excel in any role in which she was cast, from stepping in as a last-minute casting director for the film to her ever-growing natural and God-given gift as a writer, author, literary critic, and poet.

As time wore on, the measure of her talent continuously increased, as is seen by her latest work, *The Arts of Literary Criticism: Thrillers in Tanka, Book 1*, and after reviewing this beautifully unique concept of literary critique—like the proverbial onion, her layers are many levels deep and with the peeling away of each one, I believe the literary world will find that many surprises are awaiting us in the future.

As a literary critic, Cat is following her *Reviews by Cat Ellington* series and—in my opinion—is supremely qualified to create this series of enthralling and imaginative works of poetry and art. Each Tanka illuminates the premise of the story being reviewed and does so in a (uniquely) creative way. The craft necessary to create the perfect Tanka for each review is a gift that shows this artist's dedication to her craft.

As she has previously composed micropoetry pieces for *More Imaginative Than Ordinary Speech* and *Memoirs in Gogyohka,* it is a small wonder that Cat would embrace Tanka, a form of Japanese poetry song or verse that speaks to her understanding of the elegance and meaning of the age-old poetry form and how it speaks to the beauty of the written and spoken word. Learning, actualizing, and excelling in this new form is "all in a day's work" for Cat Ellington.

In the first book of this latest series, *The Arts of Literary Criticism: Thrillers in Tanka, Book 1*, Cat not only showcases her poetic mastery of Tanka but, notably, incorporates the artwork of black crows to invoke the darkness and peril of the thriller genre. As harbingers of many signs, good and evil, throughout multiple cultures, the crow is the perfect representation to accompany the Tanka micropoetry of the genre.

My previous experience as a playwright and theater critic has created a strong bond of sisterhood between Cat and me in our writing endeavors, which I have cherished. I am thrilled and honored to be invited to write the foreword for her first volume, which will undoubtedly become a distinct and valuable contribution to literary criticism.

I am pleased to be a part of this endeavor in my small way since I am fully aware that you, as the reader, will be thoroughly entertained by Cat's individualistic new take on the art of literary criticism and—if you're like me—will be reading this one again and again and looking forward to the next one – and the next – and the next …

—B.J. Patterson, Co-author – *The Making of Dual Mania: Filmmaking Chicago Style* and upcoming novel *Where Lies Live*

Literary criticism is an art form.
—Cat Ellington

Chapter One

Unveiling Merciless Women

***P**itiless is a woman who lacks morals;*

"The Great Proverbs"

The preceding Tanka of *One of the Girls*

*Life suffers these six
women who have no idea
they are convicted.
In destruction, they will drown—
with beasts in captivity.*

Analysis

Cat Ellington's Critique of *One of the Girls*

Book by Lucy Clarke
(Penguin Random House, 2022)

<u>THE INTRODUCTIONS: PART I</u>

LEAD THE WAY, O GOGYOHKA!

Gather up, woman;
The Greek islands await you.
Seek love, be in love,
But trust not your well-wisher:
For she means not what she speaks.

GIRLS, GIRLS, GIRLS—
AT A VILLA SET BY THE SEA IN GREECE.

Six English women, all friends (old and new), will spend an entire weekend at a beautiful but secluded seaside villa in Greece for a hen party to celebrate the impending wedding of Lexi Lowe. It was nice of Fen to volunteer the use of the estate—a property owned by her aunt—to the ladies for their getaway. And thus far, all is well. That is, until another bunch of uninvited guests, in the form of spiritual hosts of wickedness, arrive to wreak havoc and poop the party. And the agony these women will suffer will be like that of the sting of a scorpion when it strikes a man: for there is one who will not seek death but find it; and another who will long to die but death will elude her.

Dear reader? Shall we?

THE ACTUAL REVIEW: PART II

Six of these hens belong together;
Six of these hens are nearly the same:
But one of these hens is doing her own thing,
Now it's time to play *her* game.

HERE COMES THE BRIDE, ALL DRESSED IN ~~WHITE~~ PRIDE.

The once-famous Lexi Lowe, Lexi *Jane* Lowe, is beaming with pride as she sits in the backseat of the taxi, taking in the beauty of Greece: this trip was all Bella's idea. And a brilliant idea it was. Lexi hadn't felt up to it at first, but Bella insisted. Bella convinced Lexi that a hen weekend in Greece to celebrate the ever-popular Lexi's engagement would be perfect. Bella wouldn't have it any other way. She would not take no for an answer: Bella had the final say. And that was that.

And now they were here, gazing through the windows of their taxi at the cobalt-blue waters of the sea, partnered with a staggering landscape: the beautiful Greek island of

Aegos—which, by the way, serves as the fictional setting for this ritzy thriller.

Lexi Lowe still can't believe it. She will soon be Mrs. Edward Tollock! It's all so surreal, so fascinating. And what better way to celebrate than with her five dearest friends—in a secluded Greek villa overlooking an expanse of sea and seashore, with drinks, good food, laughter, and love?

Oh, how much fun it all seems to be in the beginning.

BELLA. A CLUCKING HEN.

Fussy, fussy, fussy. That's the hyperactive party animal, Bella Rossi. Bella is a good actress: one can never know when her smile is a frown turned upside down or vice versa. Bella never lets anyone see her sweat as she is the ultimate charmer. However, those who know her best also know this: Bella will go through Hell and high water for her friends. Bella, the mother figure, is always attentive to the people she loves. And who can fault her? She is uplifting, caring, encouraging, and a great confidante—always willing to go that extra mile. The idea for this extravagant Greek getaway? It was all Bella. The hen weekend idea? Yep, the first bridesmaid, Bella. All the food, sun, and fun? Bella. Bella wants her best friend, our leading lady Lexi, to enjoy her engagement celebration. And she will see to it that she does—no matter what.

She's a good friend, Bella. She's always there to speak positive words and pick up someone else when they're feeling low—never mind that she loves revelry and all its jollification. She's just a good person, Bella.

But she who dazzles does so with a painted-on smile.

X-WOMAN ORIGINS: FEN.

Once upon a time, Fen liked herself as a woman: she was soft-skinned, pretty, curvy in all the right places, and attracted to those of the opposite sex, who, in turn, were also attracted to her. Fen loved men. But that was all once upon a time. It only took *one* man to destroy her feminine confidence. Well, the harsh *words* of one man, that is. Now, Fen sports a buzz cut that is unbecoming for a woman. With broadened shoulders and a tight physique obtained through extensive workouts and running, Fen has bid farewell to femininity—as she now lives her sometimes stressful life as a lesbian. And however troubled their private life might be, Fen and her ladylove, Bella, play their parts well among the other hens—never letting on that anything is wrong.

But there is: if only they knew.

LIVING LIKE ~~AN A-LISTER~~ A B-LISTER.

Robyn Davies, a sidelined attorney, a new mother to an infant son named Jack, and the ex-wife of a careless adulterer named Bill, is regretful about many things that have occurred in her life, except the birth of her adored baby boy. Forced to live with her parents, no thanks to the sinkhole her once prominent life collapsed into, Robyn is flirting with depression, a heavy-laden spirit determined to destroy her.

With negative thoughts outweighing the positive ones in her mind, Robyn has become her worst enemy. No one can beat

Robyn down better than Robyn herself. Always full of doubt and self-doubt is Robyn, always willing to esteem others—like the great Lexi—more highly than herself is Robyn. In her assaulted mind, Robyn is nothing more than a B-lister now, an old dish rag who is nothing like she once was—in her heyday. Well, at least the girls thought enough of her to make her Lexi's second bridesmaid.

Always in someone else's shadow—is Robyn.

THE WINDS OF ~~SANTA~~ ANA.

Ana is the admirably self-confident (at least according to the B-list-minded Robyn) freelance sign-language interpreter who will serve her purpose as the third bridesmaid at Lexi's wedding. Or will she?

Ana puts on a confident, accommodating air, but she has doubts about the hen party weekend in Greece, unbeknownst to Bella and Lexi. Although she agreed to attend the wedding and be part of the hen party weekend, Ana is nothing, if not frugal to a fault: the cost of the trip alone is still mocking her. And Ana has to be careful of nothing. Every penny counts, and she cannot afford to trifle with one cent. Ana cannot afford to fail because her child, Luca, needs her. Panic, panic, panic; that's all Ana ever does. Ana is the type who frowns even in her sleep; she is troubled. But from where do her fears and anxieties stem? From what on earth is Ana running away? What storm system is forming in her mind, her soul?

No one can see the tell-tale signs—of the sign-language interpreter.

ELEANOR, GEE, I THINK YOU'RE SWELL. *BUT DO YOU?*

Eleanor Tollock, a gifted sculptor, is the sister of Ed Tollock and the future sister-in-law of the great Lexi Lowe. Ed encouraged his shy sister, Eleanor, to join Lexi on her hen weekend in Greece. And Eleanor agreed, although hesitantly. She has never been a crowd pleaser, Eleanor; she's only ever been the *scourge*, Eleanor; she has nothing in common with the other hens, Eleanor. And she'll only be in the way, Eleanor.

Woe is me. That is the self-inflicted motto of Eleanor Tollock. But it doesn't have to be: Eleanor is exceptionally talented. And her sister-in-law-to-be, Lexi, thinks Eleanor is pretty swell. Lexi is happy about Eleanor being part of her hen weekend. And if only low self-esteem and self-loathing will leave her be, Eleanor might be able to enjoy herself—just this once.

But they won't. The mind is a terrible thing to waste. And Eleanor's mind is laid waste to every manner of negative thought about bullies and enemies—who number many. And the death of her beloved fiancé, Sam Maine—at the hands of one of her fellow hens.

STRUCTURING CHAPTERS.

As the life of each of these women reveals itself throughout structured chapters, the reader gradually becomes entangled in a web of duplicity and turmoil: for the six women who star on the pages of this nearly expertly spun mystery thriller play their parts with unmarked precision and thus, do their creator, Lucy Clarke, respectable justice.

BACK AND FORTH THEY GO:

BACK DOWN MEMORY LANE:

Bride-to-be Lexi *never* wanted to get married. No, she was a famous dancer in her past life: a party girl sought after by many, adored by many. Her life in the fast lane was revelrous, full of lusting, notoriety, and debauchery. It was her escape. It was how she fled the old memories of her parents and their dysfunctional marriage, a marriage made in Hell. Their union had left Lexi wounded to an extent. It turned her off. For this reason, she shunned matrimony until now.

Now here she was, about to become a wife—lodging in a Greek villa with five of her dearest friends, the leading lady of a hen party in her honor. Who would have ever thought it possible? Lexi cannot wrap her head around it. The idea of marrying the man she loves—and giving birth to his child—is exciting but frightening. Oh, she can't *WAIT* to marry Ed Tollock!

Lexi. Sweet, sweet Lexi. If she only knew.

HER NAGGING GUT:

More than once, Ana questions her decision to attend the hen weekend. She misses her kid and should have saved the money she paid for the plane ticket. Confusion is undoubtedly having a field day in her mind. Ana deserves a holiday; this is true, but not here, not with these women. And no matter how hard she tries, she cannot get comfortable: she cannot sit, relax, and enjoy her book and a cup of coffee. Ana wants to go home—back to London. She should not have come on this hen weekend. And try as she might, she cannot quiet the nagging in her gut, a voice of wisdom telling her to *Go home.* Indeed, when wisdom speaks, one should listen—and heed. But does the native Ugandan, Ana? Of course not. Because she ~~wants~~ *needs* to please Lexi. Ever the man-pleaser is Ana.

Ever the keeper of a dangerous secret is Ana.

KINDRED SPIRITS:

When Fen and Robyn meet, the two women realize they have much in common. Fen and Robyn are fitness geeks and become instant friends—as the two women discover they are kindred spirits. They go on hikes together, sharing stories about their lives and getting to know one another better. But it's nothing more than platonic.

Or is it?

HELL'S ~~BELLS~~ BELLA:

A sinner from way back, Bella travels in whichever direction the wind blows. She is a Citizen of the World, and she makes no apologies. As far as Bella is concerned, she is the one forever young. Herself and Lexi, that is. All the other hens, including Robyn, are old maids. Fen is an exception. Fen is too much of a stud to be called an old maid. But Bella? She must be numero uno. Besides her two childhood besties, Lexi and Robyn, no one knows this fact better than Fen, her intimate partner. However, there appears to be trouble in paradise as Bella and Fen seem more estranged now. Opposites do not attract: Fen is heavy into fitness, but Bella shuns it. Fen likes to take it easy, but Bella rolls her eyes at any lifestyle bordering on boring. Fen is unhappy, but Bella couldn't care less, it seems, so long as *she* is. And it has been this way for quite some time: Bella is the popular one of the two, and Fen? Well, whatever. See, in Bella's prideful mind, Fen needs *her*.

They all do, even that bloody, stuck-up Ana! God, she hates her.

WHAT A PITY:

Eleanor is to this tale what the character "Hilary Small," portrayed by the English actress Olivia Coleman, is to the film *Empire of Light*. She, Eleanor, is a sad, despondent woman seeking happiness but unable to find it. Depression, the joy robber that it is, has been eating away at Eleanor's life since the death of her fiancé, Sam. Eleanor agreed to attend the hen weekend for one specific reason only. To confront the woman who murdered him.

The last woman one would expect.

TENSION-BUILDING: THE CYCLE OF VIOLENCE:

No matter how delicious the food and wine (and other top-shelf liquor) these women enjoy on their little holiday, the spirit of strife will not let them be: the arguments start.

No matter how beautiful and luxurious the seaside villa inside of which these women lodge, free of charge, the spirit of strife will not let them be: hostility seeps in.

No matter how blue and spectacular the sea on which the women sail—and in which their bikini-clad bodies swim—the spirit of strife will not let them be: the yelling, criticism, envy, jealousy, swearing, and offensive gestures compellingly rear their ugly heads.

And it goes on until, finally, something snaps. The anger is smoldering like the blast of a sawed-off shotgun, and the hidden rage imposing itself on the six women is like a rabid beast. No hatchets get buried; the spirit of pride will not allow it. Neither will the sword of the tongue—which takes pleasure in cutting them all to bloody pieces. It would have been better for these women had they all stayed home and remained in the bliss of their ignorance than to have traveled to Greece, regardless of its breathtaking beauty, only to be hurt, betrayed, deceived, and misled—with someone winding up dead.
But all who hate wisdom love death.

Indeed, murder can be treacherous at the hands of . . . *One of the Girls*.

A SMALL (BUT ALIENATED) SUPPORT SYSTEM.

The six women who dominate the pages of this thrilling (albeit somewhat inconsistent) tale—from multiple perspectives—do not need to be flanked by a supporting troupe. Their stories alone carry enough weight to fulfill the plot; nevertheless, Clarke has cast a small bundle of bit players to complement her top-billed personae, which include the following:

- Ed Tollock is the fiancé of Lexi Lowe and a man harboring many secrets. Many dirty and unforgivable secrets.

- The mother of Robyn Davies, who, though unnamed, has a speaking part and a bitter chip on her shoulder.

- Sue is a blast from the past. Bella's past. And no thanks to her being a relentless busybody, Sue unknowingly drives a wedge between Bella and Fen.

- Skipper Yannis is the native captain of the luxurious yacht Bella rents for the hens to enjoy a fabulous excursion at sea.

- Nico is an irritant who forms a rash on the self-esteem of the woman named Fen. A rash that takes years to heal.

PRELUDE TO THE CLOSING STATEMENT.

The six women (although imperfect) on these pages will make you feel, wonder, and reflect—as there is something entirely relatable about them. Unfortunately, their nearly flawless performances were left impacted by inconsistencies in the vision of their creator, Lucy Clarke. And for that reason, this literary script will lose a point in my analysis.

THE CLOSING STATEMENT.

Words and grammar fascinate me; they have since I was old enough to understand. And I was very impressed by how author Lucy Clarke expressed her story on these pages. I sometimes re-read some of the sentences in the chapters because I love the poetic way Clarke wrote them, the way the words flow so smoothly, the intellectualism they hold, and their articulateness.

Many of the words on these riveting pages are rhythmic, enticing, and inspiring. And I fell in love with their style and the personality of their expressions. Indeed, Lucy Clarke's writing is bold and fluid—boasting straightforwardness. And that I can appreciate as a reader and fellow writer.

In every story, a pro and a con must coexist. And while there are several pros to Clarke's narrative here, there are also a few cons, including inconsistencies in the storyline—that otherwise would have been meritable of five stars.

One of the Girls, nonetheless, is still an enjoyable read from its sunny outset to its overcast end—as it will transport the reader to a magnificent locale enriched with delicious food, fine beverages, and culture. It's the perfect getaway. And I would recommend it, even enthusiastically, to every reader harboring a passion for gripping mystery thrillers. Good job, Lucy Clarke. My advice to you? Learn from your cons.

Happy reading, one and all.

REVIEWER'S NOTE: It is a pleasure to thank PENGUIN GROUP Putnam, G.P. Putnam's Sons, and NetGalley for the advanced review copy (ARC) of *One of the Girls* in exchange for my honest review.

Analysis of *One of the Girls* by Lucy Clarke is courtesy of Literary Criticism by Cat Ellington for The Arts©.

DISCLOSURE: The reference to the fictional character "Hilary Small" is from the 2022 film *Empire of Light*, directed by Sam Mendes.

©2022 Quill Pen Ink Publishing. Literary Criticism by Cat Ellington for The Arts. The Cat Ellington Literary Collection. All rights reserved.

"Misled by Folly"

The preceding Tanka of *The Housekeeper*

What she used to be,
the other woman is now,
but she'll bide her time.
Then the monster will rise, rise,
and tear them all to pieces.

Analysis

Cat Ellington's Critique of *The Housekeeper*

Book by Natalie Barelli
(Furphies Press, 2019)

SLOTHFUL.

The lazy *man* says, "*There* is a lion in the road! A fierce lion *is* in the streets!"
As a door turns on its hinges, so does the lazy *man* on his bed.
The lazy *man* buries his hand in the bowl; it wearies him to bring it back to his mouth.
The lazy *man is* wiser in his own eyes than seven men who can answer sensibly.
—**Proverbs 26: 13-16**

Sadly, the same would also apply to a *woman*, including Claire, who stars as the leading lady of the chilling psychological thriller currently under review.

UNTRUTHFUL.

A false witness will not go unpunished, and *he who* speaks lies shall perish.
—**Proverbs 19:9**

Sadly, the same would also apply to a *woman*, including Claire, who stars as the leading lady of the chilling psychological thriller currently under review.

LIKE A LION(ESS) STALKING PREY.

Be sober-minded; be watchful. Your adversary, the devil, prowls around like a roaring lion, seeking someone to devour.
—I Peter 5:8

Of course, this would also apply to Claire, as she is a human host to the spiritual forces of darkness. As the pages of this dark tale begin to unfold—gradually exposing her lunacy—we obtain a first-hand look at the overweight outcast with the blemished skin and the farfetched backstory.

My dear reader? Shall we proceed?

MY, HOW THE MIGHTY HAVE FALLEN.

She hates her given name because she thinks the name *Claire* exudes beauty, stature, confidence, and elegance, qualities she now lacks. But there was a time when the world was her oyster. Her life was a dream: riches, wealth, exotic vacations, a brownstone on the Upper East Side of New York, and anything else her heart desired. She was beautiful once: slender, with a healthy head of golden hair and crystal-clear skin. She was nothing like she is now: overweight, pathetic, obsessive, and dangerously self-loathing. She is also vindictive—and vengeful.

THE ~~GOOD~~ BAD LUCK TROLL.

According to a 2020 blog post published by Maryland University (*The Evolution of Social Media: How Did It Begin, and Where Could It Go Next?*), the original purpose for the existence of social media was to "Help users connect digitally with friends, colleagues, family members, and like-minded individuals they might never have met in person." That was the intention in the beginning. Unfortunately, those seemingly innocent microblogging values have lost their way and become corrupted. Indeed, bad associations corrupt good morals. Case in point: Claire Petersen, the troubled woman who spends her lazy days stalking others (old friends and enemies) on social media platforms, trolling their timelines under the pretenses of falsehood: with only fifty-five followers on the social media platform that she uses to stalk others, the obsessed Claire claims to be a freelance publicist and Influencer. And she has plenty of stock photos exhibiting a fake lifestyle of ease to back up her lie.

Of them all, one woman finds herself in the crosshairs of a revenge plot orchestrated by the embittered Claire: Hannah Wilson. Hannah Wilson, that old, poor farm girl from Canada. The one Claire blames for ruining her once-privileged life. The same Hannah Wilson Claire accused of "murdering" both of her once-revered parents. *Hannah*.
Claire has *never* forgotten her. The pretty young Canadian brunette with the all-American act. *Hannah*. The self-seeking con artist and manipulator. *Hannah*.

She did her damage. And then she fled—back to her native Canada. *Hannah.*

Claire Petersen would give anything—even every pound of her blubbery flesh—to see Hannah Wilson again. And what Claire soon discovers is that there is truth to the old saying, "If you wish hard enough for something, you just may get it."

WELL, WELL, WELL; *THERE YOU ARE.*

Idle as she is, Claire only works two days a week—for a (married) doctor who pays her extra to show him her massive tatas. She also pleasures him with the use of her *stroking* hands: this is how she, Claire, can afford to pay her roommate, April, her share of the rent each month.
April cares enough about Claire to put in a good word for her at the BHive—a ritzy furniture store in Manhattan. The owner wants to hire a new administrator to handle the inventory and invoices and manage the company on its social media page. Claire would be perfect for the job, and April takes it upon herself to give her a reference.

Initially, the lazy Claire balks at the job offer but soon agrees to the interview. And it's a good thing she does because had Claire chosen not to head to Manhattan, she would never have seen her—sitting in the most sought-after salon on the Upper East Side: Alex Moreno's Salon. It's where the wealthiest and most famous go to be styled and coiffed. And *she* is there, among her fellow elites. A sweaty Claire looks in from the outside and sees her: *Hannah Wilson.*

Hannah catches Claire—eyes hidden behind knockoff designer sunglasses—watching. But the prey is oblivious to the predator. So much so that Hannah Wilson doesn't realize her predator has later followed her home.

NOW I'VE GOTCHA!

Her new name is *Carter*. Hannah *Carter*. And she has done well for herself—although she still feels insecure among the upper class. Hannah married a wealthy lawyer named Harvey Carter; he's a partner in a prominent law firm with clients worldwide. He looks happy in their wedding photos because he nabbed himself a prize. My, my, my. Ol' Hannah—the poor and inelegant farmgirl from Canada—has struck gold again. And she's all smiles, wearing her expensive wedding gown and fine jewels.

Claire studies the wedding photos of the Carters as she stalks the couple on social media.

Carter. The predator only knows this to be the new last name of Hannah because she deceived someone to find out.

Perfect Hannah. Will she *ever* pay the price for her ills? Will she *ever* answer for all the people she hurt—and whose early deaths she caused? Claire is going to see to it that she does.

I'LL GET YOU MY PRETTY. AND YOUR LITTLE BABY—AND HUBBY—TOO!

Claire stalks the Carters and stakes out their luxurious Manhattan brownstone until she gets her chance to

strike—like the viper she is. And she hits pay dirt when Hannah fires Harvey's longtime housekeeper, Diane.
The predatory stalker makes her move, falsely befriending the devastated Diane and picking her brain about her former employers, Harvey and Hannah Carter. And before long, she slithers into their lives—and their opulent home. That is after she steals the identity of another prospect: Hannah needs a new housekeeper—and "Louise Martin" is just the woman for the job, even though she can't cook and only pretends to do the dusting.

Claire, posing as "Louise," is finally inside. And she plays her part to perfection, coddling the postpartum Hannah and cooing her baby daughter, Mia. The plan is to butter Hannah up to win her trust and bond with the four-month-old Mia. So far, Claire's master plan is working. The point of the setup is to get the meat nice and tender before she goes in for the carving.

Claire fosters an insatiable need to destroy the woman named Hannah Carter to avenge her dead parents; she will fulfill her needs no matter what. Fortunately for her, Claire finds Hannah's secret diary. And after reading its many entries, she concludes that her new knowledge will be the perfect weapon against the lady of the manor.

See, Claire has an idea: blackmail. Claire will blackmail Hannah into public shame and get the former farmhand to admit to her past wrongdoing—before she destroys her and everyone she loves, completely and utterly.

But to execute blackmail, one needs an ace in the hole. Claire's is *Harvey*. She WILL bring Manhattan's white knight down to *her* level. Or so she thinks.

HUMAN CHESS: PLAYERS GETTING PLAYED.

As Claire sets out to destroy Hannah by driving her crazy and ruining her charmed life, she takes out her makeshift chessboard and stands her pawns on it, all of whom will play a prominent role in the unforgiving housekeeper's relentless quest for retribution.

Most assuredly, Claire will bet the (Wilson family) farm on creating a pure pawn checkmate. And the co-starring cast members who get set up on the gameboard of madness are none other than the following:

- April—Ol' gullible April—is Claire's roommate and a somewhat close confidante. Dense as an all-butter pound cake, April strikes Claire as someone who is one knife short of a cutlery set: for unlike Claire, April is not quick-witted. *Or so Claire thinks*.

- Dominic—Ol' gullible Dominic—is a good-looking photographer Claire meets in a low-end dive. The two embark on a steamy one-night stand and discover they like the romps so much that it will be an adventure to keep them going – sort of a booty-call arrangement. But unlike Claire, the flaky-as-pastry Dominic is not quick-witted. *Or so Claire thinks*.

- Diane is the former housekeeper who was fired by Hannah Carter when the former wouldn't stop reminding the latter—in so many words—that she had no place among the Manhattan elite. But on the pages of this diabolical thriller, the firing of Diane is just as well, as it opens Pandora's box to a storyline of pandemonium.

- Eryn is the spoiled (and snobbish) rich girl you'll love to hate. A witch in the eyes of Claire, Eryn only pretends to be a friend to Hannah as she covets Hannah's husband, Harvey.

Standing in the mighty shadow of the rooks, knights, bishops, kings, and queens, the weak pawns of Claire side-step across the chessboard in a desperate feat to help her capture her enemy. But there can only be *one* champion, one greater than them all. And it will take a good deal of cleverness on Claire's part to stay ahead of her adversary—as she suddenly transitions from being the head to the tail.

Here is where the cocky loses sight of the play.
Here is where the top-billed player gets played.

A CONCISE SUMMATION.

Detailed like designer wallpaper and layered like the excess fat on top of its leading lady's bone structure, Natalie Barelli's *The Housekeeper* is a twisted pretzel of tumult. The tale zigzags its way from one (seemingly brightly-lit) course at the beginning to an unlit path—the reader won't see coming—at the end. A fascinating (and complex) vision teamed with a dexterous hand opens a portal leading to a dark fictional world of intrigue and suspense: a world where fear and its colleague, hatred, hide in dark corners, where rage lurks like a rabid Pit Bull Terrier, and where depravity and perversity combine to corrupt the unsuspecting. For wherever there is a corpse, it is there that the vultures will flock.

Natalie Barelli's writing style is impressive here. Barelli keeps her script nice and lean—getting on with it and to the point, which brought about an enjoyable—and highly emotional—read. Although the cast (some you'll go from liking to loving) on these pages is small, they impact the storyline and do sufficient justice to the narrative.

If I might add, I have desired to read *The Housekeeper* for a while now—tucking it away on my bookshelf until I had time to view it. And finally, it is done.

With that, I am keen to commend Natalie Barelli on *The Housekeeper*. It *is* a well-written work of fiction. And I would most definitely recommend it to those pundits of the thriller genre.

Five . . . ~~Made~~ Maid-in-Manhattan stars.

Chapter Two

Hunting Serial Killers

O*minous is the thief of life.*

"Ruination"

The preceding Tanka of *Switch*

Don't be covetous;
for it is idolatry,
so say the Scriptures.
But this one woman will be,
and, therefore, be skinned alive.

Analysis

Cat Ellington's Critique of *Switch (Frank Quinn, #6.5)*

Book by John Lutz
(Pinnacle Books, 2012)

CAT ELLINGTON:

In the literary world of mystery and thriller fiction, the characters created by John Lutz consist of two separate yet vitally crucial groups: the homicide detectives who investigate crimes; and the depraved criminals who commit them.

The following is one of his stories.

GOING ONCE. GOING TWICE. SOLD—TO THE WOMAN WITH THE GENUINE GUCCI BAG!

There are auctions, and then there are auctions at the world-famous Sotheby's. Few know this better than Alexis Hoffermuth, the rich-and-wealthy Manhattan socialite who has just secured the coveted Cardell bracelet. Yes, she came close to getting outbid, but Alexis did it. She won the bid—snagging the diamond-and-ruby wristlet for a whopping $490,000.00. Alexis Hoffermuth got the Cardell bracelet, and Sotheby's turned a respectable profit. Alexis Hoffermuth was determined to win the bidding war: she had already gushed in the society pages about it, telling all who had ears to hear that she would buy the bejeweled bracelet. And although she fell under a nervous spell when another bidder strove to run the bidding price up—bidding by phone, no less—Alexis held her ground and won it. She outbid them all. And she would now have something (more) to brag about among her social set. Because, as they say, darling, "You can *never* be too rich or too thin."

Before long, however, Alexis Hoffermuth will be enviably slender and dead—murdered in the extravagant confines of her fifty-ninth-floor penthouse apartment—in the upper echelons of Manhattan.

REWIND.

Two days before her murder, Alexis Hoffermuth realized something: she'd been duped and fooled by a stranger.

The ditzy blonde woman who entered the limo and pretended to be so out of it that she didn't notice she was in the *wrong* limo was a con artist. It hadn't occurred to Alexis then because she was distracted by the yapping woman, but *now* she remembers. The strange woman had a Gucci bag—very similar to Alexis's. It was such a good knockoff that it did its job and fooled Alexis: the Gucci was practically identical to hers. And *that* was the play: Alexis's Gucci held the genuine Cardell bracelet while the other woman's knockoff Gucci bag held the paste duplicate. The plan was to cause a distraction while she swapped a $490,000.00

genuine diamond-and-ruby bracelet with a cheap imitation. So there. An imitation Gucci bag, an imitation bracelet, a smooth switch. Smooth as butter.

Now Alexis Hoffermuth—a demanding woman with the entire NYPD in her back pocket—is fuming. However, looking at her, one would assume otherwise. The famous socialite is a cougar and a flirt. Indeed, Alexis Hoffermuth is a woman accustomed to getting what she wants when she wants it, period. Frank Quinn (our leading man) and Pearl Kasner (who doubles as Quinn's partner and love interest) are the latest to learn this. The pair who make up Quinn and Associates—or Q&A—have been called on by Harley Renz, the police commissioner, to get on the case, stat!

After visiting Alexis Hoffermuth at her luxurious penthouse and hearing her side of the story, Frank (a fantasy conquest for the wealthy cougar, who licks her chops in his presence) and Pearl agree to investigate the case—for a handsome fee. And that starts the ball rolling.

TWO CROOKS, A CHILD, AND A CAT.

Ohio native Ida French, formerly Ida Beene, is one dynamic actress. She might be able to morph into a ditz in the blink of an eye, but this seasoned criminal is anything but a dumb blonde. Ida French is whip-smart. And Ida French can be very dangerous. Ida was perfect in her performance when she swapped the Gucci bags. She was so good that even Craig Clairmont, her partner in crime (and husband), stood back, watching in awe. Once again, the couple worked a sweet grift on an unsuspecting mark: that rich dame, Alexis Hoffermuth.

They got the genuine Cardell bracelet. They got it! And now it's time to get the dough—over $240,000.00—from the fence.

The nefarious Craig Clairmont is seemingly crazy about Ida, but he is not so much with Ida's eight-year-old daughter, Eloise, or the child's black tomcat, Boomerang. Craig is forever searching for (and finding) reasons to be irked by the whiny child (not his, by the way) and her pesky pet. But Ida loves her daughter, and there is nothing Craig can do about it. Eloise is part of the package—and that's that. No biggie. Craig Clairmont has been understanding, staying out of the child's way and keeping her out of his: peace on Earth and goodwill to all men, yadda, yadda, yadda. All remains well in the Clairmont-French household. That is until Eloise sees the Cardell bracelet on their kitchen table and snags it – to double as a collar for her beloved Boomerang.

Craig Clairmont. Until now, he had been *so* understanding and amicable. He had been *so* patient. So *very* patient. Craig is trying to get along, but an irritant to Craig is the child, Eloise. Like bleach left on his skin too long—is the child, Eloise.

DESPERATELY SEEKING BOOMERANG.

The guilty conscience of a criminal—should one exist—never fails to trip them up. It, the guilty conscience, is always careful to do two things: guide them to the impulse of desperation and then see to it that they act on it – as is the case when Boomerang, the tomcat with a $490,000.00 diamond-and-ruby bracelet wrapped around his neck, goes missing. The animal is called Boomerang for a good reason: he goes and does a U-turn right back. Boomerang is often missing in action. And until now, Boomerang's antics have never been a problem for the thieving team of Clairmont and French. Not until now.

Under any other circumstance, Craig Clairmont and Ida French wouldn't even notice Boomerang's absence. Now, though, it's a problem. The two lawbreakers are desperate; they want that bracelet back as their unscrupulous lives depend on its safe return. And when people get desperate, they do desperate things – like Ida French does when she calls the police to report Boomerang missing. But rather than some beat cop showing up to interview Craig and Ida about their missing pet, the swindling duo is visited by another couple: the law-enforcement team of Frank Quinn and Pearl Kasner.

WHAT'S THE 411?

Alexis Hoffermuth had some valuable information that many ruthless people coveted. She could've played her cards right and won the hand, but instead, she got too cute, too caught up in her false idol: her riches. The woman was sure that her wealth would rise loftily to her defense and shield her from any harm, evil person, or thing. Alexis Hoffermuth was wrong.

The more ferocious animal wanted to know what she knew. But, of course, a delusional Alexis Hoffermuth was defiant; she had no intention of revealing *anything* she knew. She would fight the beast back—or die trying. And that she did: died trying.

FAST-FORWARD.

Here today, gone tomorrow. Frank Quinn and Pearl Kasner were not that long ago speaking to Alexis Hoffermuth, and now here she was, in the same penthouse, a stiff corpse staring up at them with blank, frightened eyes. The opulence remained in the land of the living, mocking a life once lived in it—as the Queen of the palace was no longer.

But who murdered Alexis Hoffermuth in such a gruesome way? And to whom did the severed finger lodged in her vaginal tract belong?

DETECTING DECEPTION.

The murder of Alexis Hoffermuth, paired with a missing tomcat and a diamond-and-ruby bracelet worth half a million dollars, will be one hell of a case for the investigative team of Quinn and Kasler because they are all connected by one great big double-cross: a plan of deception valued at over $240,000.00.

A SMALL BUT FORCEFUL ENSEMBLE.

On the pages of *Switch*, John Lutz creates an entertaining plot of intrigue as he directs a small ensemble of players worthy of either love or comeuppance. Those who join our starring leads in this puzzling crime caper are listed as follows:

- Dr. Julius Nift is the medical examiner and a thorn in the flesh of Pearl Kasner. Julius and Pearl squabble often—as the irritating medical examiner takes a perverse pleasure in aggravating the lady detective.

- Jody Jason co-stars as an investigator-in-training studying criminal law. A natural, Jody often works on cases with Frank Quinn and her mother, Pearl.

- Harley Renz is the politically-motivated police commissioner with whom Frank Quinn has a rather unconventional working relationship. Quinn is upstanding and moral to a fault, while Renz can be too quick to take sides with corruption. Nevertheless, the two men share mutual respect.

- Jack Clairmont is the younger brother of jewel thief Craig Clairmont. Jack, who could have entered a life of law-abiding citizenship through the narrow gate, instead snubbed it in favor of a wide-and-spacious road leading to lawlessness and destruction.

- Willard Ord is the villainous crime boss who prefers to remain crouched—like a wild cat—in the shadows of New York's underworld. Boss Ord has a lot on the line, financially. And he'll be damned—to the second death—if he allows anyone to stiff him.

- Otto Berger co-stars as a book-smart thug whose two feet swiftly run to evil. Otto Berger is a man with nothing better to do than be an evil trial to his fellow human by shedding innocent (and sometimes not-so-innocent) blood.

- Arthur Shoulders co-stars as an illiterate thug whose two feet swiftly run to evil. Arthur Shoulders is a man with nothing better to do than be an evil trial to his fellow human by shedding innocent (and sometimes not-so-innocent) blood.

- Mr. Melman plays a supporting role as a crooked ex-cop and the slimy doorman at the magnificent penthouse of Alexis Hoffermuth. Mr. Melman has taken bribes since he was a rookie cop. But here, Mr. Melman takes one bribe offering too many.

A FLEETING SUMMATION.

With a little mystery here, some thrills there, and some humor here, there, and everywhere, *Switch*—book #6.5 in the Frank Quinn series—is a cunning and underhanded narrative of the novella persuasion. Infused with enough action—and a lovable leading man in Frank Quinn—to keep the reader engrossed, this fleeting tale of 85 pages makes up a story with date-stamped scene changes reminiscent of Dick Wolf's legendary *Law & Order* drama series. The only thing missing here is the famous sound effect: *Dun-dun*.

While it isn't one of the greatest novellas *I've* ever read—as I found it a bit rushed and sometimes confusing—*Switch*, penned by the illustrious John Lutz, is nonetheless intriguing, well-written, and worthy of my recommendation. Therefore, you, dear reader, should consider it so.

Happy reading, all.

"Death and Decay"

The preceding Tanka of *Dark Corners*

In the Sunshine State,
there lies a hideousness
in humanity.
A murderer with a stench,
likened to garbage, eats souls.

Analysis

Cat Ellington's Critique of *Dark Corners (Rachel Krall, #2)*

Book by Megan Goldin
(St. Martin's Press, 2023)

GETTING INTO (CAMPING) GEAR.

The Sunshine State sets the stage for this serial killer thriller penned by Megan Goldin. The curtain opens, and the cast members take their respective places and prepare to wow the reader.

As the scenes begin to roll, we travel to the grounds of a popular campsite: the Delta Springs State Forest in Daytona. Here is where a man named Bill Morrow is taking some time to relax with his family. Bill, with his wife and kids, is on a mini vacation. And the family is joined by Bill's two sisters, with their husbands and children. Bill Morrow believes he has planned the perfect getaway: the adults can enjoy the great outdoors together, and the teens can get a taste of life without video games and social media. Old school, that's the idea. After the adults pitch the tents and prepare the food, they get the volleyball fun going, and the kids soon forget about social media. The youngsters begin to relax and enjoy themselves.

Indeed, everything is calm and peaceful—until the camper van they passed on the way in becomes a problem.

The evening is pleasant but windy. And the aluminum door on that lone camper keeps opening and slamming shut. The racket has become so annoying that it's waking the kids and disturbing the adults—who are only trying to relax and enjoy their beers after a long day. When the door slamming becomes too much of a disturbance, Bill Morrow and his brothers-in-law go over to check it out. They announce themselves on arrival and call out to whoever may be inside the camper. And when the men don't get an answer, they enter the camper van. What they find inside sets off a horrifying chain of events that will shuffle in our leading lady, journalist, and famed true-crime podcast host, Rachel Krall – a woman with a sultry voice but an unknown face.

KRALLING OUT OF BED.

Rachel Krall, the host of the popular podcast, *Guilty or Not Guilty*, was exhausted after covering the lengthy rape trial of a notable swimmer in North Carolina. All she wanted to do was stay home and recuperate from the brain drain; she only wanted to sleep, sleep, sleep. And once she relaxed and settled her mind, a deep sleep arrived, whisking her away into the unconsciousness of the dream world. But before Rachel could even get a good snore in, her phone rang—jolting her up and back into the real world.

FBI Special Agent Mark Torreno was on the other end of the line waiting to take advantage of a unique opportunity: he knew that Rachel would be groggy at such an early hour. That was the whole idea: she wouldn't be thinking clearly.

Special Agent Torreno spoke fast, insisting that Rachel fly down (on an all-expense paid flight, courtesy of the FBI) to Florida. And he wanted her there as soon as possible. No explanations, no nothing. The FBI didn't need to explain. When one of its agents issued a command, one did well to heed it. And before the sun rose over the City of Brotherly Love, Rachel Krall was out of bed and on a flight.

KRALL BEFORE YOU WALK.

Former Marine and FBI Special Agent Joseph Martinez—Torreno's superior—chose Rachel because her name came up in an FBI investigation, or so they tell her. The truth is that the FBI deceived Rachel Krall. Agents Martinez and Torreno led the podcaster to believe that the agency was flying her out to Florida to work on a case, but, of course, that was a lie; the agents had other plans - plans that had to do with the goings-on behind the walls of the Central Florida Correctional Facility, where a man named Terence Bailey is serving six years. But it's anyone's guess who Terence Bailey is and what crimes landed him in federal prison. He could be a thief of the petty sort—or a cold, calculating murderer. The FBI has no clue. But Rachel Krall might know. And for this reason, the agency wants to use her.

In a slick effort to cut to the chase, Special Agent Martinez—who suspects Bailey of murder more so than a string of robberies—asks Rachel to meet with the prisoner in the hope of coercing him to confess. But why Rachel? That's simple. It's because Terence Bailey knows the legend of Rachel Krall. He's a fan, or so he claims. Complicating matters further, Bailey, only days before, slipped a hidden message to a woman named Maddison Logan: *Bring Rachel Krall to me. Do whatever it takes to find her. It's time.*

A DATE WITH AN INMATE.

Rachel doesn't know Terence Bailey—or so she claims. She denies having any knowledge about the alleged murderer. But Special Agent Martinez doesn't believe her; he has his doubts. Special Agent Joseph Martinez is nothing if not good at reading people. And he wants to know what's going on. If Rachel doesn't know Terence Bailey personally, then how does she suppose Terence Bailey knows her? Bailey is guilty as sin; Martinez can *feel* it. But the only way to extract a confession from him is to send the ever-sought-after Rachel Krall in for a visit. And what Special Agent Martinez wants, Special Agent Martinez gets.

Before long, Rachel comes face-to-face with the convicted burglar—and alleged murderer. During her visit, Rachel will notice three things about the man, Terence Bailey: his cold, blue eyes, a disdainful countenance, and a distinctive tattoo on one of his hands: an infinity symbol formed by a snake eating its tail.

THE POWER TO SWAY: A DAY IN THE LIFE OF AN INFLUENCER.

According to the Instagram page belonging to Maddison Logan, the free-spirited nomad has been nearly everywhere: the Burning Man festival, five-star restaurants, fancy bars, ritzy nightclubs, etc. The social media macro-influencer spends much of her time traveling across the country and getting into all sorts of shenanigans—while selling the so-called dream life to her many followers. Her Instagram feed is chock-full of videos and photos documenting her every waking moment. And there has never been a dull one. Maddison Logan is wild, scot-free, and full of glee. Or it at least appears that way in her countless videos and photos, accented with nothing but fun-loving hashtags.

Yes, all is seemingly good in the life of this influencer as she puts on her perfect face with a dazzling smile for her myriad of followers. But that's the thing about life filtered through social media. It can be very deceptive—as Maddison herself had been when, on the pretext of working as a missionary who visited inmates in prisons, paid one to the number one suspect in a string of sex-worker murders: Terence Bailey. But Maddison Logan would disappear hours after her social call with Bailey. And her abandoned camper—at the Delta Springs State Forest in Daytona—would be laid waste to an infestation of rats and rattlesnakes.

A CAMPGROUND OF MACABRE LEGEND.

The so-called travel influencer, Maddison Logan, has vanished into thin air, and a body found in a deep pool of mud not far from her camper has cracked open an urgent FBI investigation into her disappearance and possible murder. Many, including Rachel, believe the body found in the mud pit is the remains of the missing influencer; however, proving it will be impossible as the popular Instagrammer has no family history, nor was there any DNA found inside her abandoned camper. There was only a video of her violent abduction.

Incidentally, the abduction of Maddison Logan and the body found in the mud are not the only occurrences associated with the Delta Springs State Forest: legend has it that many people were murdered and buried there. Recently, a park ranger discovered another body tied to a tree and partially burned. The young woman was stabbed to death, apparently in an uncontrollable rage, judging by her wounds. Her name was Aysh Philips.

THE DOG AND PONY SHOW.

Maddison Logan was in Daytona for one specific reason: BuzzCon. BuzzCon is the annual convention held for the top influencers on social media, particularly Instagram. They come from far and wide to be seen by others and treated like Internet royalty. These are members of the general public who suddenly became social media "famous." At BuzzCon, fame is god. And mere obscurity? Well, whatever. There is nothing wrong with someone being an everyday person, but can one tell *these* people that? Of course not. These are those who covet fame—for doing nothing but posting photos of themselves doing outrageous things on social media platforms. At BuzzCon, the so-called influencers (or content creators, if you please) and members of their so-called pods bask in the spotlight of no shame. Using all manner of made-up jargon, they come in a variety of brand tags: travel influencers, wellness influencers, fitness influencers, fitness vloggers, and so forth.

Soon, Rachel Krall finds herself at BuzzCon, posing as an aspiring influencer, but this is another deception. The actual reason for Rachel's infiltration is to learn more about Maddison Logan and the ruthless circles in which these influencers move.

Now equipped with a fake Instagram page and many fake followers, Rachel Krall, working in a league of her own under an assumed name, dives into the saltwater with the barracudas, eels, and great white sharks, swimming a few elegant laps among them and gathering as much feed as possible.

In truth, Rachel should have packed up and gone home, as Special Agent Joe Martinez advised. But Rachel Krall cannot do that. She has to know what happened to Maddison—because, as she later learned—the missing influencer had called her for help. And Rachel Krall, being Rachel Krall, does not intend to vacate the Sunshine State without some answers.

If it is an answer Rachel Krall wants, it is an answer Rachel Krall will get. However, she may not like what she hears.

SOMETHING STINKS.

Every fictional villain has an ailment or a disfigurement of some sort. For instance, in the legendary James Bond: 007 spy film series, there is what is known as the disfigurement-villainy trope. To name a few, "Le Chiffre" (*Casino Royale*) has a nasty scar over one eye that leaks blood, "Lyutsifer Safin" (*Spectra*) has a body covered in scars, "Raoul Silva" (*Skyfall*) has a distorted jaw. And the towering character "Jaws" (*The Spy Who Loved Me,*

Moonraker) has metal teeth. Even the fictional city of Gotham has its disfigured villains: the "Joker," the "Penguin," the "Ventriloquist," Harvey "Two-Face" Dent, and the "Riddler" (with his BPD), among others.

These physical deformities expose one thing: the true spirit of evil within the human hosts – and they are terrifyingly wicked. On the pages of this complex and twisted psychological thriller, the deformity of its adversarial villain is a decaying soul that emits a body odor as repulsive as that of the murdered corpses he leaves in his wake: a stench likened to that of rotting garbage.

Our leading lady, Rachel Krall, doesn't back down from anyone, nor does she scare easily. That is until she comes to make *his* acquaintance.

VIPER BROOD.

Coiled in an infinity symbol, the snake eats its tail. There is a name for it: Ouroboros. And it is no coincidence that it keeps appearing: suspected serial killer Terence Bailey had the image tattooed on his hand, and the body extracted from the mud pit wore it. Ironically, Terence Bailey sketched a mysterious girl wearing the symbol on her pendant. And it is also on the bodies of several influencers at BuzzCon. But what do these people all have in common? And who is it that wants them all dead?

RIPE FOR THE PICKING: A WAR ON THE UNWARY.

Dark corners. They are the areas where otherworldly spirits like to hide—to go undetected by their human foes—as they hate to be exposed. And when they strike, the target never sees it coming. Because the spiritual can see the physical, but the physical can't see the spiritual. That is the advantage spiritual beings have over physical beings. And here, they are ripe to do severe damage.

Co-starring on the pages of this mind-boggling script, the characters who add another pinch of depth to an already compounded storyline include the following:

- Pete stars as Rachel Krall's producer. Pete and Rachell are like cheese and crackers: they work well together. Passionate in his craft, Pete never misses a beat as a second set of eyes and ears for Krall.

- Owen "Doc" Bragg plays a very helpful and attentive National Park Service ranger at the Delta Springs State Forest.

- Adam Derwent is the semi-retired defense attorney representing the incarcerated Terence Bailey on a string of burglary charges. Attorney Derwent is adamant that his client is innocent of murder.

- Kyle McFein stars as a retired NASCAR driver, the owner of an auto shop, and Terence Bailey's former boss. Kyle McFein loved Terence Bailey like a son until a murder charge came down the pike.

- Jonny Macon is a fitness influencer—and a cocaine-addicted hypocrite—supposedly "famous" for doing shirtless push-ups and planks and posting the videos and images to his Instagram page.

- Reni is a wellness influencer and Jonny Macon's girlfriend. While juggling her brand-new successful wellness app, Reni also finds time to mingle in a love triangle with Jonny and Maddison Logan and, according to one of her most aggrieved rivals, go in for financial fraud.

- Chad—just Chad—is a marketing executive in the cutthroat influencer business. A gossiper by design, Chad forms a communication bond with Rachel at BuzzCon and advises her concerning the pretentious influencer game.

- Zoe is a desperate fitness influencer who will do *anything* to succeed. Chasing fame and fortune—like she chases Jonny Macon—Zoe wants to win the coveted Influencer Awards with its five-million-dollar contract and streaming deal. And the wispy blonde with the Ouroboros tattoo will do whatever it takes to do so. *Whatever it takes.*

- Eric is a photographer and lapdog for the demanding Zoe, his girlfriend. Eric is wise enough to realize one thing: how will he ever be happy if Zoe never is?

- Shaz—a bit player with a minor speaking part—is a travel influencer and a blessing no one would have ever seen coming.

- Alvin Rice is the chief of the Daytona Police Department and a social-climbing bully. One of the biggest threats to the ego of the double-minded police chief is the FBI, particularly a special agent named Joseph Martinez.

- Detective Castel in homicide likes to cut corners, for the record. Rather than detecting every clue, Castel is too quick to pin criminal acts on the innocent for appearance's sake.

- Grace Milroy stars as a recovering addict and a heartbroken mother missing her only daughter, Hailey, who is feared dead.

- Mary Philips is convincing as a hotel housekeeper and a heartbroken mother missing her only daughter, Aysh, who was found dead.

- Thomas McCoy plays his part well as a friendly rideshare driver who becomes entangled with a number of his castmates and soon has to swerve around one pothole after another on the road of guile and mayhem.

IT'S—IT'S AN ENIGMA.

Several people stood to gain—and hugely—with Maddison Logan being out of the way: competitive fellow influencers, obsessed fans, and vindictive enemies. But who abducted her? And where is she? Is she dead or alive? What connection had there been between Maddison Logan and

Aysh Philips? Over one dozen people, including some prostitutes (found with their throats slashed), are deceased—the victims of a terrifying serial killer. But who is the perpetrator of such violence? And what is the motive behind their rampage?

There are many questions but few answers. That, however, doesn't deter our starring lead, Rachel Krall, from joining forces with FBI Special Agent Joseph Martinez to piece together this perplexing puzzle. Flaming sparks have been flying—like lightning bugs—between them since the first day they met. And when Rachel finds herself in the clench of murderous hands, it's either kill or be killed.

For Special Agent Joseph, er *Joe*, Martinez, the former would sooner suffice—because there is no way Joe Martinez will *ever* allow *anyone* to pull out one auburn-hued strand of Rachel Krall's hair from a secretory cavity in her scalp.

IT... IT READS LIKE A MOVIE.

With *Dark Corners*, I didn't read a book; I watched a movie—an absorbing psychological thriller spanning 78 highly intricate chapters. Rachel Krall and Joseph Martinez are sublime on these pages! And I fell in love with them as they fell head-over-heels for each other.

MY SUMMATION.

Although I considered some parts of the storyline of *Dark Corners* to be too tedious, too character-driven (in several instances), and bloated with too much information that the title could have done without, the plot, carried by a praiseworthy leading lady, still clasped my attention until its dynamic end.

Megan Goldin, an admirable writer, by the way, had a lot to say here. And understandably so, considering the premise: a psychological thriller set around a serial killer, interlaced with a hefty helping of mystery. Such a premise warrants a fair amount of detail because understanding the human psyche—and spiritual warfare—is imperative. Nonetheless, some of the body text here grated on my patience, and I felt that the narrative would have still made its point had Goldin trimmed off all of the extra fat that slowed it down.

With that, I must express my undying love for writers in general. I do believe that storytellers paint great depictions of human life. And on the pages of *Dark Corners*, Megan Goldin illustrates an enthralling world brimming with excitement, collusion, duplicity, havoc, hatred, and grisly murder. The author's words are well-written, and her creative imagination leaves a lasting impression. And that in itself commands respect.

Although *Dark Corners: Rachel Krall (#2)* was my introduction to the series starring the heroine, I also intend to view *The Night Swim: Rachel Krall (#1)*, the acclaimed mystery thriller that started it all.
In the meantime, dear reader, trust that *Dark Corners* is a respectably fulfilling read despite its minor cons. And I highly recommend it.

Happy reading, all.

REVIEWER'S NOTE: It is a pleasure to thank St. Martin's Press—and NetGalley—for the advanced review copy (ARC) of *Dark Corners* in exchange for my honest review.

Analysis of *Dark Corners* by Megan Goldin is courtesy of Literary Criticism by Cat Ellington for The Arts©.

Chapter Three

Analyzing the Wicked Nature of Man

*E*vil under the sun is evil under the Son;

"Blind Spots"

The preceding Tanka of *The Minotaur Sampler*

*A sandy picture
can be a dangerous thing
in the manner of murder.
But she, the Red Queen,
should not ask, "What have we done?"*

Analysis

Cat Ellington's Critique of *The Minotaur Sampler, Volume 7*

Book by Peter Blauner, Stacy Willingham, Anastasia Hastings, Juan Gómez, Alex Finlay, Thomas Mullen (Minotaur Books, 2022)

COMPLIMENTARY SAMPLES.

Brought to you by St. Martin's Press and Minotaur books, *The Minotaur Sampler, Volume 7* is a literary smörgåsbord of six standalone tales in the thriller, mystery, and historical fiction genres. A truly remarkable read, this well-selected assemblage includes works by a troupe of bestselling authors, namely Peter Blauner, Stacy Willingham, Anastasia Hastings, Juan Gómez-Jurado, Alex Finlay, and Thomas Mullen.

Guaranteed to clutch its reader, *The Minotaur Sampler, Volume 7*, is compiled of the onsets of each narrative featured and is led by the epic *Picture in the Sand*, authored by Peter Blauner. Now, without further ado, I am ready to analyze the set. Dear reader? Shall we?

- **PICTURE IN THE SAND by Peter Blauner**
  Genre(s) Historical Fiction / Mystery Thriller

My rating: 4 out of 5 stars

~~GOD~~ ALLAH OF WAR.

Alex Hassan was a promising young man—once. His Egyptian-American parents only wanted the best for him. They worked hard and gave Alex the best life they could; Alex never needed anything. He and his younger sisters, Amy and Samantha, had all the trappings a child could want from their parents: love, devotion, attention, and a firm hand to guide him along the path of life. Alex and his parents endure in America regardless of the spirit of racism, which often targets them, resulting from their race and faith; nevertheless, the family can look past the cruel barbs when they perceive their good fortune: Alex's father is an executive at Chase, and his grandfather is a respected entrepreneur. They have done well in America. And to show their gratitude, the family flies Old Glory high on the front porch of their quaint American home.

Oh, if their friends back in Egypt can see them now.

Nay, America has been good to the Hassans—until now. On the day those two twin towers fell in New York City, America (the Beautiful) frowned her face into a scowl of ugly scorn. Forgetting her reputation for being the great Melting Pot, America became as bitter as vinegar, and her tongue protruded from her mouth like a double-edged sword, sharpened by the fire of her belly. With it, she spoke to slay her adopted Muslim children; they were no longer welcome among her own. The sharp tongue of a nation in suffering and mourning cut through many carotid arteries as it spoke to the Muslim immigrant from the abundance of its heart: *Go back to the desert, Osama.*

Alex Hassan, a chemistry and video production major, had worked hard, kept abreast of his studies, and finally gained acceptance to an Ivy League university: Cornell. It was only one more stitch in the patchwork of the American dream. And Alex was happy. However, that quickly changed after the FBI arrested and jailed his father for acts of terrorism. Of course, the elder Hassan was not a terrorist; he only had the *same name* as an actual terrorist. The FBI apologized, and Alex Hassan's parents accepted the apology and forgave the offense. But Alex never did. *And he never will.* Especially not since his family lost nearly all they had because of it. Enough was enough.

Unlike his parents, Alex Hassan has a different spirit: a vengeful one that fosters the philosophy of an eye for an eye and a tooth for a tooth. And on the pages of this gnawing sample of *Picture in the Sand,* Alex Hassan will make a decision—and no one, not even his reformed grandfather, film fan Ali Hassan, will be able to modify his conditioned mind. No matter how many emotional letters his grandfather writes to him, Alex doesn't care; he wants revenge. According to Alex Hassan, "The world is a battlefield. And we must all choose sides."

And so it happens. Abu Suror (formerly Alex Hassan) chooses a side: martyrdom. Indeed, Allah would approve. Alex Hassan has found his destiny. He will join the Muslim Brotherhood in the struggle for freedom.

His militant recruiters in Syria patiently wait to exact retribution: woe unto the enemy—*America*.

Is it possible to salvage a misguided soul adrift in a sea of revenge? The true struggle has only begun.

- ***ALL THE DANGEROUS THINGS* by Stacy Willingham**
  Genre(s): Psychological Thriller / Mystery
  My rating: 5 out of 5 stars

THE DISAPPEARANCE OF MASON DRAKE.

Starring Isabelle Drake, *All the Dangerous Things* sets the stage for a psychological production of true crime—produced and directed by a puzzling mystery: the kidnapping of a baby boy only one year ago.

The child is named Mason, and our leading lady, Isabelle Drake, plays his grieving mother. The night Mason Drake disappeared, the weather had been warm and rainy, a gentle breeze blowing in, refreshing the nursery. Isabelle and her husband, Ben, were asleep in the adjoining bedroom. And neither had heard the window to the nursery opening or an intruder entering: this is at least the story the Drakes told the authorities when they realized their only child, Mason, was gone.

In the year since the disappearance of Mason, Isabelle has not enjoyed a good night's sleep. Insomnia is now the master, and she is its slave. Coffee and eye drops try in vain to provide comfort, but their efforts are only so far-reaching. Isabelle Drake is now a human Luna Moth, a creature of nocturnality. How she stays afloat is anyone's guess, but she does, although desperately. The human body needs rest, but Isabelle can never sleep longer than the duration of a catnap. Most recently, she gave a keynote speech at TrueCrimeCon, an annual event for True Crime fanatics held on the West Coast. And even though the case of her missing child remains unsolved, Isabelle commits to attending every year to keep those interested parties up-to-date on any breaks in the investigation. Thus far, it is routine for Isabelle to merge in and out of character as she stands on stage, speaking and looking out at the perverse people who almost gleefully take pleasure in the misfortunes of others. It's always the same old speech—at which she has become a pro.

Her baby is missing, stolen from his crib in the middle of the night. And her husband has left her to carry the burden of losing their only child to abduction alone. Exhausted, Isabelle hasn't slept too many winks since then. Her body is breaking down, with her eyes succumbing first. The irreparably broken blood vessels exhibit a subconjunctival hemorrhage—resulting from a lack of sleep. And to say the least, it's getting worse.

Any mother would be prone to suffering emotional stress after such a trauma. And it's no different with Isabelle Drake. Or is it?

Something awful is troubling Isabelle. She works hard to keep her composure, but there is something about Isabelle. Is she hiding secrets? Does she know more than she's revealing? A woman such as herself, who has garnered the attention of millions in the aftermath of Mason's disappearance, is not keen to go unnoticed by the likes of off-shoot media outlets.

Take Waylon Spencer, for instance. Waylon Spencer is a true-crime podcaster who (just so) happens to be booked on the same flight as Isabelle (in the seat next to hers) on her way home—to Savannah, Georgia—after TrueCrimeCon. He starts a conversation with Isabelle, eventually offering her his business card and inviting her to appear as a guest on his show for an interview. Perhaps it is only a coincidence? Isabelle keeps to herself on the flight. But she holds onto his card, which may not have been a good idea because if Isabelle Drake knew the real reason Waylon Spencer wanted her to rehash that horrible night of the abduction on his podcast to millions of listeners, she would have discarded his business card and never saw him again. But when one is under a spell of delusion, the same is not thinking clearly.

Is Isabelle Drake not unlike all of the other mommies? That is what Waylon Spencer would like to know. And he doesn't intend to sleep on it.

- ***OF MANNERS AND MURDER* by Anastasia Hastings**
  Genre(s): Historical Fiction / Mystery
  My rating: 4 out of 5 stars

TAKE *HER* ADVICE—AND DIE.

In the world of nonfiction, we have Dear Abby, Ann Landers, Claire Rayner, and E. Jean Carroll, to name a few.

And in the world of fiction, there is Miss Hermione—the best of the best in the advice columnist business. Whatever the problem might be, Miss Hermione has a solution. And whatever the question is, know for a certainty that Miss Hermione will have an answer, as this is her claim to fame. Miss Hermione is the premiere agony aunt in the British Empire, advising all who inquire, no matter the time of day.

As the tie-backs open pinch-pleated Victorian curtains to reveal her charmed life, the reader will learn firsthand that not all is as it appears in 1885 London—the era of Aunt Adelia, famously known as Miss Hermione.

The 40-year-old Adelia is as elegant as she is sassy. She believes in living it up: on a whim, Adelia can easily pack up and go (without a second thought), which is what the renowned agony aunt is doing when she summons her dear niece, Violet, into her home library to give the younger woman the news. Adelia is about to be whisked off on a pleasure trip—yet another exciting excursion courtesy of her paramour, Hamish MacGill. And it is her will for Violet to oversee the *Miss Hermione* advice column while Adelia is away. Of course, Violet is caught out and dumbfounded: there is no way Violet can write an advice column. She just can't. And in no uncertain terms, she argues to convince her dismissive aunt of that. But Adelia will hear none of it. It is *her* way or *no* way.

Ironically, until now, the true identity of Miss Hermione was a mystery: no one, except Adelia's loyal housekeeper, Bunty, and a few others, knows that she is the famous advice columnist: this, too, throws Violet for a loop. Notwithstanding, the hypocritical Adelia wins the match against Violet's objections, and Violet has no choice but to honor her legendary aunt's request. So there. It is said and done: Violet will write the advice column until further notice. Violet will now be Miss Hermione, a revered figure who has never been apt to practice what she preaches.

A hot cup of tea has a way of bringing out the sunshine and chasing away the clouds. At least it does for Violet, as only one cup, made for her by Bunty, serves as a little liquid courage. Violet is ready to become the substitute for Miss Hermione.

The first of many letters she must answer comes from a newlywed woman who has written to Miss Hermione before: she pleads with Miss Hermione to answer her inquiries about how she should carry herself as a new wife. Also, the writer of the letter has self-esteem issues and believes she must do whatever is necessary to please others. Never herself, only others, especially her husband. The woman signs her letter, *A desperate but hopeful wife*. And in turn, Miss Hermione dubs her "Desperate but hopeful." Unfortunately, the advice given to the desperate housewife did nothing to calm the choppy waters in her marriage. And when she sends the advice columnist a second letter, its spirit is even more anxious than the first: the woman informs Miss Hermione that the matter is far from settled and that the situation has grown grave.

The woman—whom we soon learn is named Ivy—goes on in her letter, telling Miss Hermione that she suspects someone is trying to kill her. Ivy admits she has a good idea who they are, those who want her dead, but she neglects to name them in her correspondence; however, her letter does include clippings and photos of those she suspects are plotting to kill her. The frightened woman has drawn circles around each one; the details are shocking. Violet confers with Bunty about whether or not Violet (posing as Miss Hermione) should publish the letter. Bunty doesn't fancy the idea and encourages Violet to dismiss the anxious woman's accusations as rubbish. But does Violet? Of course not. And we wouldn't have a suspenseful murder mystery, an arousing little whodunit, to keep the pages turning if she did, now would we, dear reader?

It's not until Violet visits Ivy that the substitute advice columnist realizes the rabbit hole, or grave, for that matter, goes deeper than she could have ever imagined.

Trust that the suspects in the heinous murder of Miss Ivy are the ones you will least expect.

- ***RED QUEEN* by Juan Gómez-Jurado**
  Genre: Crime Thriller
  My rating: 3 out of 5 stars

THE INSPECTOR AND MRS. ~~JEFFRIES~~ SCOTT.

On the pages of this sleazy crime thriller, Madrid, Spain, serves as the setting for a hard-boiled storyline of international intrigue.

Inspector Jon Gutiérrez lives with a bull's eye on his back. Not only is he a target because he's gay and lives with his mother, but Jon is also on suspension (without pay) from the force for several offenses that range from falsifying evidence to obstructing justice. Jon is perceived—by his captain and peers, among others—as a corrupt cop, although Jon insists nothing is further from the truth. There are things Jon's captain and fellow officers don't know about him, including *why* he did what he did. But *Jon* knows. Desiree Gómez, also known as either Desi or Sparky. *She's* the reason why. Desiree is a 19-year-old prostitute who Jon will go to great lengths to protect—even if that means destroying her pimp, the same pimp who beats her to a pulp without a conscience.

Jon risked his career and life to help the pitiful hooker who lacked gratitude. And to make matters worse, Jon's captain seems to be looking for *any* excuse to rid the department of him. Honestly, it's not because Jon did something no other cop has ever done; it's because Jon is gay.
If matters couldn't get any worse than they already are, Inspector Jon Gutiérrez is staring down four to six years in the Basauri prison for his "abominable" misdeeds. They're all out to get him: his sanctimonious captain, the homophobic district attorney, the prostitute Jon tried so hard to protect, the pimp Jon framed, and the angry inmates Jon had a hand in helping to imprison. Not surprisingly, Jon is now at a fork in the road: he may go to prison, and his 70-year-old mother may never see him again, should she perish before his release. The dark thoughts infesting his mind desire to break his spirit and perhaps nudge him to suicide, but Jon has too much faith in life to take the so-called coward's way out. He's contemplating his next move when a shyster called Mentor makes his entrance. For Jon, Mr. Mentor can (and will) wipe the entire slate clean and have all the charges dropped—but there's a catch: our

leading lady, Detective Antonia Scott. Soon, Inspector Jon Gutiérrez will curse the day he meets her. Or he will bless it.

Now, one could ask, who is this mystery man called Mentor? And what power does he have to influence print and visual media? What influence does this man, Mentor, have over law enforcement? Why is Antonia Scott and her expertise in criminology so important to him? The shady figurehead wants to use the misfortunate Jon Gutiérrez, knowing he has a card to play against him: Jon will do as the man called Mentor asks, or Jon will go to prison. It's as simple as that.

In time, Jon delivers Antonia to the man called Mentor as instructed – but there is no way the organization for which Mentor works will allow Jon Gutiérrez to walk away so easily. Surely, Jon should have known better. But then again, naivete has never been a reliable subject to advise on wisdom or the principles thereof.

His delivering Antonia Scott to Mentor is just the beginning of the seemingly endless troubles about to befall Inspector Jon Gutiérrez. And he will need his wits fully intact to maneuver through a double-crossing labyrinth of treachery.

- ***WHAT HAVE WE DONE* by Alex Finlay**
  Genre(s): Thriller / Mystery Thriller
  My rating: 5 out of 5 stars

Three blind mice, three blind mice,
See how they run, see how they run...

THE SCOPE OF A WOMAN: JENNA.

Jenna is a woman who has it all, at least on the surface.

The lovely housewife is married to a much older man, a tax attorney named Simon. And they have two daughters from Simon's first marriage: Willow and Tallulah, nicknamed Lulu. Willow, the oldest, is not fond of her stepmother, Jenna, but Lulu, on the other hand, is a bit more hospitable. Jenna is giving it her all with Willow, but the girl won't budge: as far as Willow is concerned, Jenna will *never* replace her mother. Simon's first wife succumbed to cancer, and with time, he started living again—after meeting Jenna on Match.com.

A wealthy clan, the family lives outside of Washington, D.C., in a home teeming with opulence. Simon's friends and family conclude that Jenna only married Simon for his money, but unbeknownst to them, Jenna already has a vast sum of her own money—tucked away in a private little Swiss bank account. Jenna. She is good at keeping secrets from all of them.

Friendly but friendless and often lonely, Jenna is a great actress. She plays the hell out of her role as a doting suburban housewife—with a loving husband and two precious stepdaughters: this might be her new life, but Jenna's past has never gotten over her. It has searched high and low to find her place, and its efforts were not fruitless. After its resurrection from the dead, Jenna's past has come to pay her a call, rapping about old times and arousing an old lust – an old bloodlust.

For Jenna has never had to atone for her sins – until now.

DONNIE DANGER? YOU'RE IN DANGER.

Sex, drugs—too many, in fact—and rock & roll have done severe damage to not only the liver but also the soul of the man named Donnie Danger. Once a powerhouse in music, selling out arenas and whatnot, the band for which Donnie served as the frontman, Tracer's Bullet, is now reduced to playing cruise ships to pay the bills.

Donnie Danger, the band's iconic guitarist, was only sober for three months before an evil agent, posing as an adoring fan, arrived to be a thorn in his flesh: the time was a perfect opportunity as Donnie recently learned that his best friend, Ben, was found murdered. Donnie Danger fell off the wagon soon after, and things changed, as Tom Kipling, the band's new frontman, is none too pleased, and all of Donnie's bandmates, except Pixie, despise him. They hate him, but they need him because Donnie, one of only two original band members, is the primary reason the band of has-beens stays booked in the first place.

Donnie is trying to keep his head above water, but it's a challenge: his best friend is dead, and Tom Kipling—who writes all of the band's songs—wants Donnie out. Says Tom Kipling: "It's him or me." And with that, Donnie knows it's over. But what is he going to do now? He needs the band like he needs a life preserver. Speaking of which, a life preserver would come in handy, as Donnie will soon realize. Another "adoring fan" approaches Donnie Danger on the quiet deck of the ship as he stares out at the vast darkness, drinking to forget his problems. Donnie assumes she wants an autograph—across her cleavage, which is customary. But the stranger doesn't want his John Hancock. She wants Donnie Danger to jump off the ship deck into the deep, cold ocean below. When he laughs it off and takes her for a joke, she brandishes a loaded gun and counts to five before shoving him overboard.

Donnie Danger, an aging rock god, has never had to atone for his sins – until now.

WHO KNOWS THE MINE OF NICO?

Nico is the executive producer of the reality TV series
The Miners. The title is fitting enough for a program centered around its cast members venturing into many of the world's coal mines.
Roger (call him "Maverick," or else) is Nico's star. And before he found "fame" on *The Miners*, Roger was an obscure member of the general public—as were others of his like, meaning so-called "reality TV stars."

Nico detests Roger, but the annoying idiot is his "star" and main moneymaker. Yes, because of the massive success of *The Miners*, Nico is bathing in money. And he can overlook every diva-like ego so long as the cash keeps streaming in. Nico is the king of all executive producers in the reality TV industry. Andy Cohen, who? Nico is untouchable—or so Nico would like to believe.
Nico has a great deal to contend with, as does Davis. Davis is the mean-spirited network executive who covets Nico's

job. The man is like a pounding migraine in Nico's temporal lobe, but it's nothing the executive producer can't handle. If truth be told, Nico has endured worse: lone sharks, bookies, that sort. Perhaps Nico's meeting with Roger—down in the mine—may produce some drama he can use for the show. You know, ratings and all that.

The fact that there can never be enough drama in reality TV is the *only* reason Nico accepted Roger's invitation to meet underground in the mine. Under any other circumstance, Nico would have dismissed the demanding man-child. So when the rickety elevator lowers its passenger into the coal mine, Nico stands there, waiting. However, there is only one problem: the passenger who exits the elevator is not Roger; it's someone else. And that person has come but for one reason: to kill Nico. The mission? Blow him to bits.

Nico, the famous reality TV executive producer, has never had to atone for his sins – until now.

THEY MUST SUFFER TO THEIR LAST BREATH.

Although it's been years since former friends—and Savior House group home residents—Jenna, Donnie, and Nico went their separate ways, the trio have history, ugly history. Our three starring leads have moved on, left that history behind, and forgotten it. But there is one who hasn't. This one remembers what they did. And for their wicked feats, they must be held accountable. Destruction must befall them. On their journey to the realm of the dead, they must suffer to their last breath.

- ***BLIND SPOTS* by Thomas Mullen**
  Genre(s): Crime Thriller / Mystery / Science Fiction
  My rating: 2 out of 5 stars

OUT OF SIGHT.

What happens when every human on Earth dreams the same nightmare at once? On the pages of this sci-fi crime thriller, authored by Thomas Mullen, the terror of it becomes real when a mysterious plague strikes the globe and blinds every man, woman, and child with one life to live.

It's been seven years since the inexplicable virus crippled the world and caused macular degeneration. Scientists created a name for it: The Blinding. No one was immune; every human alive contracted it. The direct symptom was impaired vision. Everyone soon lost their sight, and the world they all once knew plunged into darkness. There were many theories about how the virus germinated and the ground zero of its origin. Was it a bioweapon let loose by China? Could it have been the Russians? Was it climate change? Or a parasite? Something in the water? No one knew. The virus came like an hour of trial upon the entire world. And since The Blinding, many have had their faith tested—for seven long years.

Enter Officer Mark Owens, our leading man and a detective in Major Crimes. As this narrative opens to display the world on its pages, Officer Owens, along with his partners, Officers Jimmy Peterson and Safiya Khouri, is on a stakeout. The nightclub, *Slades*, is more than a place to go dancing; it also serves as a shell company for drug deals and gun runners, not to mention prostitution. PTSD be damned. The show must go on. And a good night's rest still must eschew the wicked.

Equipped with new technology, people can live and perform their daily duties as they once did before the virus claimed their sight: Vidders are small metal discs implanted on everyone's right temple. This device relays GPS, radar, and every diversification of visual data to the occipital lobe's visual cortex, compensating humans for their permanent blindness. In the case of law-enforcement officers, Vidders go one step further, allowing them to see through walls with thermal imaging: this can work not only in their favor but also against them. Officer Mark Owens learned this the hard way. It nearly cost the veteran cop his life when the leader of the criminal organization Owens and his department were working as a task force to bust became suspicious of the detective's advantage. And in the commotion of the raid, Owens, with a damaged Vidder, nearly shot Jimmy Peterson to death – as Peterson was being used as a human shield by a man named Slade, the unit's prime suspect.

In the end, though, they both survived. They always do. But their luck—at catching criminals and keeping the streets safe from all forms of criminal activity—is about to run out.

Are Owens and Peterson the good guys? Or are they a double team of trigger-happy corrupt cops abusing the integrity of the badge in a world without sight?

For if the blind lead the blind, will they both not fall into a ditch?

- That concludes book 6 of *The Minotaur Sampler, Volume 7*. My summation is as follows:

SUMMARIZING THE MAIN POINTS.

I must say that *The Minotaur Sampler, Volume 7*, was quite interesting. The six tales collected here had individually unique personalities that ranged from choleric to melancholic, ill-tempered to courageous, and adventurous to energetic. And maneuvering from one plot to another, and then another—all in one book—reminded me of the first time I read *Night Shift* by Stephen King. The only difference, as far as the comparison goes, is that *Night Shift* is a collection of nineteen books. And when you have that many characters following different plots, one must maintain focus. And that I did.

As the titles in this compilation are only samples, I based my ratings on prose, plot, character, and pace. And of them all, *What Have We Done*—authored by Alex Finlay—was perhaps my favorite sample, followed by *All the Dangerous Things* by Stacy Willingham, both of which I rated five stars. With *What Have We Done*, I was on the edge of my cozy reading seat, so immersed in the plot that when I reached the end of the sample, I cursed—out loud. Indeed, I do foresee viewing this title in its entirety.
All the Dangerous Things also had a rapid pace and a riveting storyline that grabbed my interest and held it from start to finish. And I look forward to completing it as well.

The two titles I rated four stars are *Picture in the Sand* by Peter Blauner and *Of Manners and Murder* by Anastasia

Hastings. These are both great books that show promise as complete works. The two narratives are well-written and pleasurable—to an extent. And while I would recommend them to any reader interested in epic tales or historical fiction, this duo of snippets was a little too slow for my taste.

Red Queen by Juan Gómez-Jurado comprises the only narrative I rated three stars. Unfortunately, the anecdote was not impressive enough to bowl me over, although I would still recommend it to my fellow readers. If you love international crime thrillers with a feisty heroine at the helm, this one might be your perfect cup of Earl Grey.

Thomas Mullen's *Blind Spots* could have been much better. The sci-fi thriller earned two stars on my rating scale by a hair's breadth. The excerpt was nothing short of slow-moving, inducing extreme fatigue. And I couldn't wait for its four chapters to end. Mullen's writing here appears lazy and practically amateurish. And too many broken sentences give the impression of a rush job. In addition, too many characters run into each other without much of a good rapport. And if these four chapters indicate what the entire novel will read like, I have no interest in ever completing it. Notwithstanding, I wouldn't go so far as not to recommend it to fans of the sci-fi thriller genre—as everyone has a preference. And as the old expression goes, 'To each his own.'

As I have not read his other work besides *Blind Spots*, I cannot judge the quality of Thomas Mullen's bibliography as a collective. He just failed to wow me here.

With that, dear reader, I would recommend *The Minotaur Sampler, Volume 7*, to those who fancy a little variety—despite its minor cons, which its pros outweighed, mind you. It is an engaging anthology that will set the mood perfectly on a rainy day. And I am sure you will enjoy it. Thank you, Minotaur! And happy reading, all.

REVIEWER'S NOTE: It is a pleasure to thank St. Martin's Press / Minotaur Books / Macmillan—and NetGalley—for the gift of an advanced review copy (ARC) of *The Minotaur Sampler, Volume 7*.

Analysis of *The Minotaur Sampler, Volume 7*—co-authored by Peter Blauner, Stacy Willingham, Anastasia Hastings, Juan Gómez-Jurado, Alex Finlay, and Thomas Mullen—is courtesy of Literary Criticism by Cat Ellington for The Arts©.

"The Dawn of AI"

The preceding Tanka of *The New One*

A menacing child
has folly bound up in them,
that the rod won't cure.
But in time, AI will snap;
and with it, the mind of Man.

Analysis

Cat Ellington's Critique of *The New One*

Book by Evie Green
(Berkley Publishing Group (Berkley), 2023)

CONJUNCTION JUNCTION, WHAT'S YOUR *DYSFUNCTION?*

Alone in her family's quiet caravan in the English unitary authority of Cornwall, an agitated Tamsyn Trelawney is in a reflective mood. She is worried about the daughter she once held dear but who is now like a form of rottenness in her bones. Scarlett. The fourteen-year-old menace. Tamsyn thinks about her husband, Ed, who does his best for their family, but no matter how hard he tries, his efforts never seem good enough. They were a happy family once; Tamsyn has the photos to prove it. But now, it's different. Much more so than it ever was. Now they hate each other. They don't talk to one another; they shout, screaming at each other, *hating* each other, and *hating* their poverty.

The family of three lives in a caravan on a campsite, surrounded by other individuals and families in the same dinghy—anchored down by impoverishment and faithlessness. Tamsyn sits, thinking about her family and how it came to this. She calls Scarlett and leaves another message, and then another, and then another. But she gets no answer. The down-beaten mother wonders where her rebellious daughter is and why she is not yet home. And when Tamsyn calls Ed, he tells his wife that he'll find their daughter. He does. And when father and daughter arrive home, the screaming starts again: the swearing, fighting, anger, and rage, stimulated by self-hatred: a dysfunctional family trying to fight against unseen forces—and losing the battle.

They are tired of their lots in life and tired of each other. And they want it to end. They want out. Tamsyn wants the daughter she once had. Ed wants a better wife and daughter. And Scarlett wants wealthy parents, not poor ones. But as the old saying goes, You don't miss your water until the well runs dry. And before it's over, Tamsyn, Ed, and Scarlett will regret the wicked deception of their heart's desires.

Dear reader? Shall we proceed?

THE HIT-AND-RUN.

Folly hates wisdom to the core because wisdom reminds it of all it lacks: good sense, prudence, and foresight. Folly is a rebellious, willful spirit; it loves to scoff and wallow in its mire of delusional ignorance. It also loves to deceive the flesh and lure it into a self-destructive nature. Folly takes pleasure in misguiding human beings. And where it concerns Scarlett Trelawney, the mindset of idiocy is having a field day.

Young and unlearned, Scarlett's mind is under fierce assault - so much so that the child, totally blindsided by anger and its co-conspirator, rage, cannot see her way clearly to distinguish the forest from the trees. And it is here that the roaring lion, disguised as an invisible entity, breaks forth to lead her astray, as it will seek to devour the hard-hearted child in the form of an accident, a hit-and-run.

AN OFFER TOO GOOD TO REFUSE.

The accident happened so fast that Scarlett didn't know what hit her. And for the past twelve weeks, she has been in an induced coma, wedged between the land of the living and that of the dead. In only one week, her insurance will be exhausted, and if she hasn't awakened by then, the life-support machines that are keeping her alive will shut off. Scarlett's parents, Ed and Tamsyn, are aware of that, but so are Nurse Maya and a shadowy man named Johann—the latter an agent sent by Old Scratch to be a poisonous thorn in the flesh of Ed and Tamsyn Trelawney.

The offer Luca Holgate made Ed and Tamsyn was too good to be true. It was also convenient. Because as their comatose daughter, Scarlett, lay, possibly dying, the stressed-out and penniless couple had no choice but to accept the generous, albeit mysterious, proposal. And even though Tamsyn *knows* something isn't right, she eventually agrees to forge ahead with the plan despite her initial objections.

THE GRAND ILLUSION—AND DELUSION.

GENEVA, SWITZERLAND — At VitaNova, a high-tech but obscure clinic nestled in the heart of Geneva, scientists and medical doctors are embarking on something remarkably innovative. A small team of medical professionals has invited Ed and Tamsyn to be part of a unique clinical trial, the so-called Reanimation Project. It will serve as a second chance for the defeated Trelawney family. VitaNova—The Tyrell Corporation (of *Blade Runner* fame)—of this tale will fly Scarlett to Geneva and provide her with the best care possible. And Ed and Tamsyn will never want for anything—again. The stench of poverty that once wafted from the family of three like musty armpits will suddenly vanish—to be replaced by the fresh scent of money and extreme wealth.

As promised, the opaque folks at VitaNova are lavishing the Trelawneys with all that one's heart could wish. Scarlett's room at the facility is as luxurious as can be; Ed and Tamsyn can see the Swiss mountain range from the windows in the suite. And their new home is even better: a humongous flat with a top-of-the-line coffee system, fully-stocked refrigerators, and wine selections, along with walk-in wardrobes with only the finest attire and footwear and a rooftop terrace to die for. VitaNova has also provided Ed and Tamsyn with preloaded phones that allow the couple to access unlimited funds—deposited on the devices—to pay for whatever they need. Tamsyn, by now accustomed to expensive perfumes, makeup, and the best hair designers, has even joined a chess club and taken up yoga and courses in French. No longer emaciated from a lack of food, Tamsyn is curvy and healthy. And her skin glows with radiance. It's all too good to be true. But at the same time, it's difficult to resist. Ed is all for the "reanimation" project, but something in Tamsyn is still not sitting well with it. Motherly intuition, if you will. No matter how free and comfortable her new way of living is, Tamsyn is still leery—and doubtful. However, with time, Tamsyn softens around the edges and begins to blend in with her coveted environment.

Humans, they say, can adapt to anything.

The Trelawney family was once a poor, angry, and desperate unit, holding on to survival by a string. No one knew this better than Old Scratch, who sat crouched, biding his time. From his invisible advantage, he watched the family voraciously. And when he saw the Trelawney family on the brink of collapsing from the weight of hopelessness, Old Scratch, working through a slew of wicked human operatives, pounced again—like a wild beast.

INTRODUCING SOPHIE. *THE NEW ONE.*

Her brain is a human-AI interface, but her human part is all Scarlett Trelawney. Sophie—Scarlett's middle name—is a cyborg created by VitaNova. Her purpose is simple: she exists to be a completion to the Trelawney family, while her original prototype, Scarlett, lies unconscious in her induced coma. Sophie was programmed to protect *Ed and Tamsyn*. And that is just what the Man-made mechanical being intends to do.

Sophie's personality comes from the brain of her human twin, Scarlett, combined with software coding. Sophie has no memories of her life at age twelve because Ed made a special request to delete those—and VitaNova granted his wish. Scarlett Trelawney was at her worst during her twelfth year of life, and no one wants to remember that. But Sophie is the new and improved Scarlett. Sophie will be everything Ed and Tamsyn ever wanted in a daughter, everything Scarlett was once: friendly, intelligent, happy, eager to learn, and loving.

So far, so good.

Ed and Tamsyn are in love again, and their new life is a dream come true, never mind all the cameras and listening devices installed in every room of their fabulous new apartment. Added, their reanimated daughter, Sophie, thinks she's the *original* Scarlett. And Ed and Tamsyn are content to allow her, er, *it*, to believe the delusion.

What Ed and Tamsyn forget to remember, however, is that Sophie was not *born*; she was *made*—by scientists. Unlike a natural human being, she has no spirit or soul. There are cameras implanted in her retinas, and the cyborg is more intelligent than they give her credit for: this is how Sophie knows about the secret visits to VitaNova that Ed and Tamsyn pay Scarlett, among other things. A cunning mechanical being, Sophie learns about Scarlett, her original self, and desperately wants to see her. Sophie is now beginning to contemplate without articulating, knowing that she must continue to play the game and be a good daughter. The computerized mind of the child is thinking along these lines: *There is only room for three in their family: Ed, Tamsyn, and Sophie. Not her twin, Scarlett. Sophie can never allow Scarlett to recover – lest she returns to destroy it all.*

With that, a murderous spirit enters the machine.

Ed and Tamsyn have convinced themselves that everything is good, happy, and well. But the cyborg, Sophie, is constantly thinking, her thoughts growing more sinister. Meanwhile, the original Scarlett slowly returns to consciousness, emerging from the dark place of her coma with sheer defiance. To prove it, when told by a familiar voice that she was not going to get better, Scarlett hoarsely replied, "Yes, I am!"

Whatever she may think, the cyborg Sophie is about to meet her match—with her human twin.

SUSPICION—TORMENTS MY HEART.

Living a better life than before aside, Tamsyn is beginning to grow suspicious of Sophie, a gradual building of doubt. Sophie is too eager to meet Scarlett, her human twin that she has already attempted to kill, unbeknownst to Tamsyn. And something about Sophie's too-enthusiastic-and-impatient aura is making Tamsyn eerily nervous. Besides that, Tamsyn suspects that Ed is having an affair with his beautiful colleague, Lena. He's hardly ever home anymore, and he's now lying to her—all the time. *Could he be?* Tamsyn, more often than not, wonders. And when she follows him—confidentially—to learn the truth, what Tamsyn finds will devastate her to the core of her inner being: for the taste of *Honey* is sweet in the mouth of Ed but bitter in the belly of Tamsyn.

THE INEVITABLE MALFUNCTION.

There are many distractions. And that's a good thing as far as Sophie is concerned because she plans to murder Scarlett. The cyborg has even hinted at it to the original human—mocking Scarlett's weaknesses. She is going to kill if it's the last thing she does. And a still-injured Scarlett won't be able to defend herself because Sophie is much stronger than her, naturally. Sophie *hates* Scarlett, and she *knows* things. But what secret does Sophie know about her twin, Scarlett? The horror movies Sophie selected for Scarlett to watch during her recovery at home? Why was *I Know What You Did Last Summer* included in the bunch? Scarlett wonders about this, but the answer eludes her. Sophie, the cyborg, on the other hand, was programmed to perform her duties adequately. And if she wants to avoid the Incinerator at VitaNova, she had better do so.

Here is where the nightmare that someone wouldn't wish on their worst enemy becomes real, and once it does, there will be no safe place for the humans to run to. Here, the Trelawneys will have to pray that their flight is not in winter – especially not during winter in Switzerland.

IN GOOD COMPANY: THE SUPPORTING PLAYERS.

Everything you ever thought you knew about AI is minuscule compared to the megalomaniacal lunacy on the pages of Evie Green's *The New One*.

The spirit of its body text takes on a form that lies with a straight face and deceives with the hoodwink of a robotic eye: for it is within this tale that those of a herd mentality fall as one by the edge of a blazing sword, and those of arrogance receive their reward, each according to his doing: for when human beings exalt themselves to the level of playing God, the same *get* played—every time.

Adding to an exceptional cast of leading characters, Green incorporates a small but dashing bundle of supporting—and bit—players to complete her literary script. The troupe rounds out the ensemble as follows:

- Maud is Tamsyn's best friend and the Trelawneys' neighbor. A spunky old gal with a heart of gold, the 70-year-old Maud now lives in widowhood after the death of her wife, Ally.

- Jimmy Trelawney co-stars as Ed's distant but ever-reliable brother. Even if Jimmy *is* against VitaNova and its human cloning ventures, he loves his brother, Ed, and vows to stand with him and support his decisions.

- Luca Holgate delivers an applause-worthy performance as a top scientist at VitaNova and a least likely ally of a resistance.

- Nurse Poppy plays a small but vital role as an assistant on Scarlett's medical team.

- Aurelie, the Trelawneys' chic new neighbor at their new flat in Geneva, befriends Tamsyn and Ed but refrains from making the couple privy to her dangerous secrets.

- Sabastian Quinn is an alleged conspiracy theorist and one of the greatest threats to the enemies of Mankind.

- Miss Lena co-stars as more than a pretty face and delectable figure; she's the voice of reason for The New Ones—a new community of Man-made humanoids.

- Jasper Mack plays a restaurant worker and the human equivalent of a snake. Jasper is Scarlett's worst nightmare, and Sophie is his.

- Jasveen Singh is a highly-regarded doctor at VitaNova and a beloved angel in the flesh.

THE CLOSING STATEMENT.

A thoroughly intriguing—and sometimes frightening—sci-fi thriller, *The New One* is a tale that took me that much longer to complete because I deliberately wanted to extend my time with it, as everything I look for in a good thriller stands to attention here: excellent writing, rapid pace, suspense, convincing characters, entertainment, and a fascinating subject matter.

Evie Green continued to impress me with her appreciable knowledge of the science behind human cloning, the same called somatic cell nuclear transfer (SCNT). Green did her homework, and the storyline here is evidence of it. However, on the contrary, the novel does have its cons, though they pale in comparison to its pros. I disagreed with the notion of harmony between Man and machine, which probably wouldn't play out well in the real world. Also, while I felt that Green added more than the required pinch of fantasy to the recipe of her plot, which left an unpleasant aftertaste, I understood the spin of ideology. Rendering credit, the author desired to tell a story centered around AI (Artificial Intelligence) and human cloning and the horrors sure to ensue when human beings interfere with the laws of nature. And she did that quite well.

In comparison, *The New One* is Vincent & Brackley's *Humans* meets Rod Serling's *The Twilight Zone*. And if you, dear reader, are a fan of sci-fi thrillers and enjoy either of those series, then I am sure you will find this title nothing short of entertaining. And while *The New One* didn't quite make it to five stars on my rating scale, even still, I would generously recommend the title to my fellow readers—with commendation.

Happy reading, all.

REVIEWER'S NOTE: It is a pleasure to thank Berkley Publishing Group (Berkley) for the advance review copy of *The New One* via NetGalley.

Analysis of *The New One* by Evie Green is courtesy of Literary Criticism by Cat Ellington for The Arts©.

Chapter Four

Exposing the Lie of Falsehood

*T*error *is the reward for those perverse from the womb.*

"The Way of Death"

The preceding Tanka of *Symphony of Secrets*

*One talent can look
at another's ten talents
and seethe with envy.
Then envy will lead the way,
so a hand might be bloodied.*

Analysis

Cat Ellington's Critique of *Symphony of Secrets*

Book by Brendan Slocumb
(Penguin Random House, 2023)

```
The following three-part analysis
contains language which some readers
may find offensive. I would strongly
advise viewer discretion.
—Cat Ellington
```

• *The Overture*

DEFINITION BY DESIGN.

Composer
(kəm-pō-zər)
noun

A person who writes music—as a professional occupation.
The term traditionally indicates composers of Western classical music or those melodists who are composers by

occupation. Many composers are, or were, also proficient performers of music.

Genius
(jēn-yəs)
noun
Someone who is exceptionally intelligent or creative—whether generally or in some other particular respect.

According to its description in *Wikipedia, Genius* is "a characteristic of original and exceptional insight in the performance of some art or endeavor that surpasses expectations, sets new standards for the future, establishes better methods of operation, or remains outside the capabilities of competitors."

So, this leads me to ask the following:

WAS *HE* A GENIUS? OR WAS HE *NOT*? THAT IS THE QUESTION.

Frederic Delaney, considered by countless people as one of the most revered composers of the twentieth century, never mentioned any of those inspirations for his acclaimed operas, and there was a good reason for it: he plagiarized nearly all of them. Now, some people would disagree; they would even fight—or worse, *kill*—to defend the honor of the late Frederic Delaney, especially if it meant maintaining their livelihood: for the works of Frederic Delaney have made tens of millions of dollars, all of which are lain upon a snobbish foundation of sand daring the rain to descend, and the floods to come, and the winds to blow and beat upon it.

Frederic Delaney the Great is a god as far as those who benefit from his estate and namesake are concerned. And he WAS a genius, so say the masses. But some beg to differ. And these would include our two starring leads, who will team up to uncover the truth. However, it may cost the relentless meddlers their lives.

Dear reader? Shall we?

THE PRESENT

~~BURNING~~ **BERNING WITH ZEAL.**

Professor Kevin Bernard Hendricks, or "Bern," is a well-respected musicologist and professor at Columbia University. It's perfectly alright to admire someone for their work, but Bern's obsession with the late composer Frederic Delaney and the Foundation named in his honor borders on false idolatry. While it is unnecessary, Bern feels indebted to the Delaney Foundation. And why is that? Well, it is because Bern, a native of Milwaukee, grew up poor, living below the poverty line until Frederic Delaney or, rather, the Delaney *Foundation* saved him and gave Bern a shot at redemption. Yes, the poor, Black kid from the 'hood made good.

Thanks to the instruments donated by the Delaney Foundation, Bern learned to read and play music and studied the art of composition, mastering the craft with practice. The Delaney Foundation believed in Bern when no one else did.

While most of his friends from the old neighborhood were either dead or in prison, Bern was ushered through an open door of opportunity and guided down the corridor leading to success and a better life. And it's all thanks to the Delaney Foundation. Therefore, Bern is always eager to please and appease where it concerns anyone—or anything—bearing the name Delaney. Bern would abandon his mother on her deathbed if it meant his assistance could keep the Delaneys in existence.

Indeed, Bern, conditioned to a fault, will always be Johnny-on-the-spot for the Delaney family. No one knows this better than Mallory Delaney Roberts, the great-niece of Frederic Delaney and one of the last of his surviving descendants. Mallory Delaney Roberts is the Executive Director of the Delaney Foundation, situated in midtown Manhattan, only steps from the prestigious Juilliard School in New York. So when she contacts Bern to inform him about some (highly) sensitive documents that pertain to the estate of Bern's idol, Frederic Delaney, the professor is intrigued.

Not inclined to discuss the matter over the phone, Mallory insists that Bern visit the Delaney Foundation (all expenses paid) to discuss her findings in person. And Bern, so emotionally subdued in his passion for everything Frederic Delaney, rather than discerning the seriousness in Mallory's tone, asks if she's found a lost piece of music. Without waiting for an answer, the giddy Bern convinces himself that the Foundation has finally found one of Frederic Delaney's most prized, albeit lost, compositions: *RED*. Mallory doesn't answer; she only insists on seeing Bern as soon as possible and that Bern sign a confidentiality and nondisclosure agreement. And what Mallory Delaney Roberts wants, that she gets.

With his leave of absence arranged by the Delaney Foundation, Bern hauls it to New York – as this could be it, the biggest score of his life. Bern will be the most celebrated musicologist alive if this is what he thinks it is!

But will it be? And will Bern be ready for what awaits him?

Way too trusting, Bern. Perhaps he should have read the NDA before signing it, Bern.

THE BELLE OF THE BOOGIE-DOWN BRONX.

Bern, good ol' Bern, is ecstatic about the task at hand: restoring one of the great Frederic Delaney's lost masterpieces. Bern was even content to sign the nondisclosure agreement that the Delaney Foundation insisted on before starting the coveted project. But once he delves into the century-old documents, the dependable professor soon realizes his need for an assistant. Sure, Mallory Delaney Roberts could have provided Bern with a gofer with one snap of her expertly manicured fingers, but Bern has a preference.

Enter Eboni Washington, a free-spirited computer security specialist, pizza fanatic, and native of the Boogie-Down Bronx. Bern and the awesomely intelligent Eboni go back to when the two attended Columbia together, Eboni then writing code for operas. She is the first person Bern thinks of when considering a comrade to work with him on the Delaney project. But one thing Bern knows for sure: Eboni

Washington, a maverick entrepreneur with her own computer security systems company, won't come aboard cheap. The Delaney Foundation will have to pay top dollar for her services—whether Mallory Delaney Roberts, a woman Eboni can't stand, likes it or not. Because where Bern won't dare offend, the blunt Eboni will. She does not bite her tongue, Eboni Washington, nor does she conform well, Eboni Washington. The belle of the Boogie-Down Bronx *knows* her business. And she is always one step ahead of her foes. No one, not even Mallory *Delaney* Roberts, is a match for Eboni Washington. And now that she and Bern are back together, conjoined as a double team, let the team work on the lost Frederic Delaney masterpiece, *RED,* begin.

THE JoR-DASH.

It isn't easy trying to piece together the puzzle of a one-hundred-year-old mystery, but that is the dilemma in which Bern and Eboni find themselves while trying to decipher the hidden meanings in Frederic Delaney's fascinating Doodles. And the enigma grows more perturbing when Bern's sharp eye catches something every other eye missed: the word *JaR* written in a neat little corner of the sheet music.

Deeming the detail interesting enough to research, Bern and his dynamic partner, Eboni, hunt down any clues that might give them insight into what the *JaR* means. They search and search, and then BAM! Thanks to Eboni's inability to fail at her job, she and Bern soon learn that the *JaR* is *JoR*. The writing on the one-hundred-year-old document was fuzzy, and they mistook the *o* for an *a*. Now Bern and Eboni must find out what the letters mean. And to do that, they must travel to Oxford, North Carolina.

SEEK, AND YOU SHALL FIND.

It wasn't until Bern and Eboni, while in Bern's office hacking into the Delaney Foundation's computer system, saw the archives and hit pay dirt.

Bern and Eboni saw her pretty face in the photos first. She was seated off to the side, but she was still visible. The celebratory atmosphere in the photograph (from 1920) betrayed the world fame of the man who had been named Frederic Delaney: the trip to Europe aboard the Queen Mary booked for the entire Delaney Party, the food and drinks, the smiles, the applause, and the cheers—all frozen in time. The guest list of eight names included hers: Josephine Reed, or *JoR*, Frederic Delaney's mysterious Dark Lady.

Josephine Reed. Now Bern and Eboni had a name—and a face.

THE TRUNK SHOW.

After researching Josephine Reed further and unearthing her family tree, Bern and Eboni jet it south to Oxford, North Carolina, the mysterious woman's birthplace – because it is there that the Reed descendants still dwell.

Bern and Eboni can track down the Reed clan from the information they obtained about Howard Reed, the brother of Josephine. The two soon meet Earlene Hill, a lovable woman and the daughter of Howard Reed, and her two daughters Myrtis and Sandra—along with some other Reed family members—and before long, another missing piece of the puzzle turns up: an old steamer trunk, dusty and hidden in the basement of Earlene's quaint home. When they spot Josephine's painted white initials on the trunk's lid, Bern and Eboni, especially Bern, can't open the one-hundred-year-old luggage piece fast enough. Hearts race as Bern struggles to pry the lock loose. And when he finally breaks it open, they find a treasure trove: the Compendium of the late Josephine Reed. It's all there: her doodles, her manuscripts, her notations, her melodies—ALL of it; hundreds upon hundreds of pages, illustrated with masterpieces. Bern can barely believe it. *What on earth?*

Eboni and the Reed-Hill family form an instant bond. And after Bern offers to pay the family—a nice sum of money—for the trunk, he and Eboni depart with it in tow. Of course, Earlene and her children agree to visit Eboni in New York, and hugs and cheek kisses get exchanged. Bern and Eboni now have proof that Frederic Delaney was nothing more than a fraud, a liar, and a thief. He was no musical genius at all. But Josephine Reed had been, although she had never received any honor or recognition for the magnificent musical works that *she*, and not *Frederic Delaney*, composed.

Bern and Eboni are relieved and happy; a couple of smart cookies, especially Eboni Michelle Washington. Until now, they have covered their tracks—to keep the Delaney Foundation off their trail. But they made a mistake when Eboni insisted on flying down to Oxford, North Carolina, on a plane owned by the Foundation.

The powers that be on its Board of Directors know about the trunk. But Bern and Eboni are oblivious to their knowledge. Here is where they get too cute—and trip.

• *Part Two*

THE PAST BEFORE THE PRESENT

SONGS IN THE KEY OF LIFE.

The year was 1918. The city was New York. And Freddy Delaney was part of a jazz combo featuring Bobby, Red, and band leader Eli, who fostered resentment toward the outfit's only White member, Delaney. She would often frequent the smoky joint known as the Alibi Club and sit in the shadows, away from the stage, listening to the guys as they rehearsed their numbers and transcribed the sounds of the world around her. The offensive Eli liked to call her "Crazy Jo," but her name was Josephine. And she may have appeared quiet and childlike in her ways, but she was brilliant, jam-packed with mesmerizing musical ability. Josephine Reed may not have come across as the sharpest knife in the cutlery set, but the woman was amazingly clever. When Josephine Reed transcribed what *she* wanted to hear, her melodies were remarkable, unlike anything anyone had ever heard.

No one understood her strange language; for example, *The orange is in (the) black and green*. To many, the phrase sounded crazy, but once Josephine translated it into chords, the music was beautiful to hear. The lady could compose a masterpiece just by hearing the sound of a car engine, feet on the pavement, a knock on a door, a shape, a color. Each sound or object, to her ears, was a chord. And she would compose what she heard in the sounds of life; her musical interpretations were nothing short of genius. Josephine knew music. And she recognized mistakes, even those that the White guy named Freddy continuously made during the rehearsal.

If it had been up to Eli, the marginally talented Freddy Delaney would've been a goner—out of the band because Eli didn't think that Freddy, who irked Eli with his sloppy piano playing during rehearsals, could cut it: Freddy, on the other hand, was desperate for the approval of his gifted Black bandmates, and he desperately wanted to be liked by them. Indeed, the Indiana native would have done anything to win their affection. But he couldn't get it right in the sets: he was always late, two bars behind on the change. Josephine pointed out as much. And when Eli asked her to show Freddy the ropes, Josephine, in her frazzled dress, sat down at the piano and played the tune perfectly: this was the beginning of life with Freddy and Josephine: *A Riding of the White Torrent.*

EBONY AND IVORY LIVE(D) TOGETHER IN (IM)PERFECT HARMONY.

The White guy, Freddy, was so enthralled with her gift of music that he took her home to his studio apartment, a shabby spot but a place with four walls, nonetheless. In exchange for a floor pallet, meals, and a bathroom down the hall, Freddy wanted Josephine—a vulnerable but brilliant adult—to teach him how to flourish on the piano so that he would become a better musician. Because he, after all, had something to prove. Freddy Delaney was no songwriter; his boss, the nasty and racist Mr. Ditmars, let him know that in no uncertain terms. Freddy Delaney might be a musician, but his talent is mediocre at best: he pays his rent working as a song plugger for the music publishing entity of Ditmars & Ross.

Freddy Delaney. He couldn't get ahead if a strong wind blew along to push him forward. But he could always go home to Josephine. She would have a hot meal waiting along with the extraordinary music she'd written. They went on this way, and Freddy even got Josephine a job (filing and cleaning) at Ditmars & Ross—after practically begging on his knees: for Mr. Ditmars initially didn't want a "coon," a "monkey," working in his place of business. But Freddy's begging won out. And before long, one humiliation after another, an idea entered the mind of the desperate and self-loathing Freddy Delaney: take one of Josephine's songs to Mr. Ditmars and sell it—under the name of Freddy Delaney, of course. Because Freddy will never tell Ditmars that Josephine wrote the music, knowing full well that the White publisher would never pay for music written by a Black woman, ergo the sole authorship credit given to Delaney.

Bring Back the Moon, an instant hit, was the composition that started it all. By selling the works of Josephine Reed as his own, Frederick Delaney is well on his way. And while Mr. Ditmars might be skeptical—earlier likening the song plugger's songwriting to garbage and trash—he goes on paying Freddy for the exceptional music.

When did such a marginally talented song plugger become a musical wunderkind? Mr. Ditmars figures Freddy just got lucky.

ILL-GOTTEN GAINS.

With time, Delaney's forename would transition through several alternate spellings: *Freddy, Frederick, Fred,* and *Frederic.* Time, in cahoots with songs composed by the uncredited Josephine Reed, had also cleaned him up, put some money in his possession, escorted him to Bergdorf Goodman—a department store at which Frederic Delaney would otherwise have *never* been able to shop—and introduced him to fame: *worldwide fame.* Sure, Delaney contributed lyrics to the songs, but his lyrical content paled in comparison to the music written by Josephine. It was the *music* the people wanted to hear; the lyrics were just in the way. Nevertheless, adding them to the compositions soothed Frederic Delaney's guilty conscience.

Buying Josephine one new dress and one pair of new shoes also serves as a salve for the blisters resulting from the burning hot coals upon his head: Frederic Delaney is raking in tons of money with his new music publishing company built on the back of Josephine Reed's magnificent compositions. Delaney even takes Josephine along on a tour of Europe, telling her that he's doing it all for *them* and not only *himself.* But the man is a liar: Delaney takes the most for himself and gives only a token amount to Josephine. He lives the good life (at her expense) while Josephine is ignored, overlooked, and limited by her race in a biased, wicked, ungodly, and racist society. Josephine misses the old

Freddy and longs to have things back to how they were—when the two lived in the run-down, one-room New York studio. What's worse is that Freddy keeps making her promises he never delivers on. There's always an excuse. *There's always an excuse.*

The world praises Frederic Delaney as a musical genius, but a musical genius he is not. Frederic Delaney is, however, a double-minded man. And a double-minded man is unstable in ALL his ways.

THE LORD OF THE (OLYMPIC) RINGS.

The genius (the *real* genius) Josephine Reed was always inspired by the sounds and objects of life when composing what she wanted to hear in her musical works. But her biggest inspiration, the one that exploded into a phenomenon more exciting than all of its predecessors in her Compendium, came after *Fred*, no longer *Freddy* but *Fred*, took her to the Olympic games during their trip to France. Motivated—and fascinated—by the design of the Olympic flag, Josephine began to transcribe. And the result was the masterwork, *The Rings of Olympia*. Five operas were composed to represent the rings on the Olympic flag: *GREEN*, *BLUE*, *BLACK*, *YELLOW*, and *RED*—the latter which would come back to haunt the descendants of Frederic Delaney, as well as his fraudulent legacy, 100 years later.

Frederic Delaney, not surprisingly taking full credit for composing *The Rings of Olympia* with four of its internationally acclaimed operas, would stand alone as the most preeminent American composer of all time. He effortlessly rode the wave of a lie with *GREEN, BLUE, BLACK,* and *YELLOW*. But when it came to *RED,* he got pitted. Frederic Delaney—whose reconstruction of the score was sloppy and amateurish—couldn't complete *RED* without Josephine Reed, the actual creator of the five operas. And when he sensed that his ill-gotten wealth, riches, fame, and the love of the world stood in the path of jeopardy, Frederic Delaney, who'd long ago sold his eternal soul, felt compelled to summon the serpent of old for one final favor — leading the way to destruction and agonizing regret.

-

BACK TO THE PRESENT

THE UNVEILING OF TRUE SPIRITS.

In the words of the late, great Dr. Maya Angelou, 'When people show you who they are, believe them the first time.' An advisory of sorts reflecting simple wisdom, yes? Unfortunately, Bern Hendricks hadn't allowed such wisdom to be his guide at the outset. And regret now jeers at him as he stands before those he had once believed to be his friends and benefactors: the Board of Directors at the Delaney Foundation.

The bodily waste hits the fan when Mallory Delaney Roberts summons Bern to meet with Delaney Foundation Board members, including its chairman and Mallory's cousin, the octogenarian Kurt Delaney. Bern can sense the ugly spirit of racism buzzing like a wasp ready to sting: Kurt

Delaney is on the cusp of calling the Black *man* with the Ph.D. a *boy*; Bern can detect it in the older man's tone. They know something; Bern can *feel* it. The members of the board were discussing him—and Eboni—before his arrival. And his veins are already filling with ice-cold blood as his heart loses its rhythm. Finally, Kurt Delaney asks Dr. Hendricks: What was in the trunk? And then another blow: Tell us about Josephine Reed.

The spirit of fear hauls off and punches Bern in the head with all its might, leaving his mouth agape, albeit speechless, and his brains scrambled.
The professor will not answer their questions; he should play dumb, which he does—until they show him the photos on their big-screen monitor. The Board of Directors knows who Josephine Reed was. They also know the contents of the trunk Bern (and Eboni) bought from Josephine Reed's descendants. They want the trunk; 'It is the property of the Delaney Foundation!' Kurt Delaney scolds. He and his board are giving Bern (and his *girlfriend*, Eboni) 24 hours to bring the trunk to the Foundation. But will Bern and his whip-smart gal pal, Eboni, hand over the precious steamer trunk with its incriminating evidence in favor of Josephine Reed but against Frederic Delaney? They wouldn't be on the run for their lives if they intended to do so, now would they?

The threat of danger waits—while grinning maliciously—at every turn. Is there *no one* in the back pocket of the filthy-rich, powerful, ruthless, sinister, immoral, intimidating, and murderous Delaney Foundation? Dr. Bernard Hendricks and Eboni Washington are about to learn firsthand that hurting rich people by turning them into poor people is not an option for those on the hunt for their blood.

THE PERFORMING ENSEMBLE.

The supporting players on the pages of this mind-blowing thriller weaved into historical fiction fall into sync beautifully with our top-billed cast members and are as worthy of applause as said starring leads – and the reader will be either pleased or displeased to make their acquaintance. Rounding out our talented ensemble is none other than the following:

- Jacques Simon co-stars as a fellow musicologist and ornery colleague of Bern Hendricks. Jacques Simon fosters the desire to be the alpha male in his and Bern's professional environment.

- Stanford Whitman is a crooked attorney, the chief in-house counsel at the Delaney Foundation, and a man the destroying angel can't eliminate fast enough.

- Mona Keltner stars as a hard-nosed reporter with professional ties to *The New York Times.*

- Cliff Rich portrays Frederic Delaney's secretary. Cliff Rich is a bigoted racist who, despite his employer, Delaney, would spit in the face of Josephine Reed if he could.

- Brian Etting plays Frederic Delaney's arranger and yet another enemy-minded toward Josephine

Reed—the real musical genius and the reason for his having a job in the first place.

- Samantha Bell stars as the granddaughter of a Ditmars & Ross founder and a blessing in disguise.

- Tom Pendleton plays his merciless part well as a member of the Delaney Foundation board. Like Stanford Whitman, Tom Pendleton is a man the destroying angel can't eliminate fast enough.

- Miles Turpin portrays a struggling pianist, a fellow song plugger at Ditmars & Ross—and a doomed man who knows too much.

- NYPD Officers Fields, Fry, and Dickson, along with their superior Detective Kirdahi, portray crooked cops on the take—and flunkies on the Delaney Foundation payroll. A disgrace to the badge, this quartet of numbskulls deserves to be dumped alive in a swamp teeming with ferocious crocodiles.

- Lauren Weber shines in her role as a cut-throat and no-nonsense attorney that it wouldn't be wise for anyone on an opposing legal team to trifle with.

The previously listed ensemble of bit-part and supporting players is never out of tune with our starring leads. And together as one, the castmates render flawless performances on the well-written pages of this tale.

The Outro

MY CONCLUDING SECTION.

An extraordinary work of fiction penned by the gifted Brendan Slocumb, *Symphony of Secrets* is an anger-inducing, perplexing, intelligent, complex, emotional, evocative, entertaining, revelational, thrilling, romantic, and thoroughly suspenseful high-speed time warp from past to present!

Blessed with a spirit reminiscent of John Grisham's timeless masterpiece, *The Firm*, the high-octane *Symphony of Secrets*—a powerful historical fiction thriller spanning 100 years—is guaranteed to take hold of the reader, pull them to the edge of their seat, and keep them glued there from beginning to end. I found it quite challenging to put this book down and even more disheartening to complete it. But much like all good things, the story had to end. And in this case, on a heart-pounding note (pun intended). What a splendid read!

The writing style of Brendan Slocumb impressed me tremendously, as did his vast knowledge of classical music and the history of the genre. A musician himself, Slocumb, with *Symphony of Secrets*, has composed—in an allegro tempo—a fabulous tale of noteworthy intrigue. And I will never forget this literary script or any member of its cast. Trust, dear reader, that Brendan Slocumb's *Symphony of Secrets* is nothing if not worthy of my loftiest recommendation.

Five D-major-scale stars!

REVIEWER'S NOTE: It is a pleasure to thank the publishing teams of Knopf, Vintage, and Anchor, as well as NetGalley, for the advance review copy (ARC) of *Symphony of Secrets* for my reading enjoyment and honest review.

Analysis of *Symphony of Secrets* by Brendan Slocumb is courtesy of Literary Criticism by Cat Ellington for The Arts©.

"The Dirty River ~~Seine~~ Sin"

The preceding Tanka of *What the Neighbors Saw*

The river runs cold
to hide decomposition,
as the guilty freeze.
Let the bird out of its cage,
and watch the cold river rage.

Analysis

Cat Ellington's Critique of *What the Neighbors Saw*

Book by Melissa Adelman
(St. Martin's Press, Minotaur Books, and Macmillan Publishers, 2023)

CONTENT WARNING: This review contains language which some readers may find offensive. I would strongly suggest viewer discretion.
—Cat Ellington

A "CALLOUS POEM" SHALL LEAD US:

For Woe is a pity,
And none too pretty—are its ugly cries
Bitter from the menace of bane,
Like cold, acid rain—
Do the tears pour down from its lying eyes

For the one who eats the dust,
The same is serpentine:
Nipping at the heels
Of the gumshoes—
Who have no abounding fields to glean

They are barren,
Laid waste—

Full of dead men's bones,
And arrogantly unchaste,
As they play host to hypocrisy
And keep company with misery

Whiffing the savory aroma
Emanating from the pit of its den,
Their crooked mouths water
For the succulent taste of sin—

With needle-like teeth—
All the better to gnaw off the flesh of the blameless,
These are those beneath—
Who prove themselves to be savage, grievous, and shameless

They are cunning; they are perverse
They are vindictive; they are— for better or worse
They are the poisonous potion
Of a witches' brew;
They are— the stars of the murderous mystery thriller
Currently under review

Dear reader? Shall we go get 'em in the proceeding analysis? Well, alright, then, let's do it.

THE RIVER OF DREAMS: STARTING OVER.

Our leading lady, Alexis Crawford, has been on the come-up for practically her entire life. The high-powered—and *high-salaried*—attorney has paid more than her fair share of dues, and she is worthy of the better life she pursues. The senior manager of a small consulting firm (and a law wiz), she shares her life with her husband and fellow attorney, Sam Crawford, the couple's toddler son Caleb, and little Caleb's Honduran nanny, Elena. They do alright, but Alexis wants more—and she will have more.

As the pages of this spiteful tale begin to turn, we meet the Crawfords at their residence—a quaint little row house in the heart of Washington, D.C. The day is hectic as Sam (working overtime to nab a partnership role at his prestigious law firm) and Alexis are moving quickly to make it to their appointment on time. They have an open house in River Forest, an exclusive community of multi-million dollar homes offset by lush forests and the scenic Potomac River. Alexis is desperate for an upscale change, but Sam? Not so much. At least not in the beginning. But he'll come around.

Or at least Alexis, the voracious social climber, hopes the grumbling bastard will.

A RIVER OF JOY: BUYING 51 SHADOW ROAD.

The house that will soon belong to the Crawfords is a humongous million-dollar-plus fixer-upper that the couple plans to buy as is. 51 Shadow Road; that's the address. The 5,100-square-foot estate (boasting five bedrooms and four-and-a-half bathrooms) needs a ton of renovation. But Alexis and Sam can't imagine the modifications the property will require (or the doctor's prices attached) until they close and move in. That was the first error of judgment, but no one seemed to care at the time. Alexis was so gung-ho about buying the home—to get away from the urban environment of their row house—that she pressed Sam to secure the sprawling estate in its current condition. Plus, it was a steal; the previous owners could not *wait* to get the house off their hands. And so they went, they saw, they bought. 51 Shadow Road (a glorified albatross) now belongs to the Crawfords.

Sam might be grunting, but Alexis—pregnant with baby number two—is beaming. She has finally done it! Alexis Crawford, *of all people,* has finally reached the pinnacle of society. Oh, if her poor, neglectful mother (*ol' hateful bitch*) could see her now, she'd turn face down in her potter's field grave! If all the friends Alexis never had could see her now! If all her *enemies* could see her now! Rich, wealthy River Forest, here she comes! Alexis Crawford made it!

She's somebody!

A RIVER RUNS THROUGH IT: THE NEW COMMUNITY.

Who wouldn't want to live in a spacious Cape Cod Revival in an exclusive community inside the so-called Beltway? Sam thinks the new neighborhood is too expensive and says as much, but Alexis is content to brush off his negative opinions because, one, they need more space for their growing family; two, their piggy bank is only a dollar short of morbid obesity; and three, they can use the change of scenery. They can do this, and they will. They are *doing this;* Alexis won't have it any other way. Plus, the Potomac River flows right through their new neighborhood; they can hear the relaxing sounds of rushing waters from their patio. It doesn't get any better than that. Here, in River Forest, their happy place awaits. Or so Alexis thinks.

Alexis also makes a mental note that she and Sam will need a more top-end vehicle—as their humble Honda Civic Hatchback, compared to the Mercedes, BMWs, Porsches, and Jaguars cruising the paved roads of the neighborhood, looks like a broken-down piece of junk.

Already, worldly temptation is luring Mrs. Crawford to hurry and catch up with the Joneses—or, in this case, the Bards.

BLONDE RIVER: MEETING THE BARDS.

There's "Bennifer," there's "TomKat," and then there's *TeddyBlair*.

Blair and Teddy Bard are the so-called "Barbie" and "Ken" of River Forest. Blair is a talented interior designer, and Teddy, a highly successful businessman, is also a long-standing member of the Virginia House of Delegates. The sparkling couple share three (secretly unwanted by Blair) children: Whit, the incompetent cross-country runner; Jamie, the soccer standout; and Rob, the badminton player. These three are all blond/blonde like their parents and troubled to various degrees. The Bards are outside their massive, jaw-droppingly beautiful home doing rainy-day yard work when they spot an odd, out-of-place-looking pair with a small child touring the neighborhood. Here, Blair Bard makes the acquaintance of her new neighbors, the Crawfords.

Alexis takes note of the striking blonde woman instantly—as the woman is the type that always seems to have more on the

148

ball in life than women like Alexis. Those types were always the most popular girls who led privileged lifestyles financed by their wealthy families, while urchins like Alexis could only attend a good college on a scholarship. They were the mean girls, the hateful girls, the spoiled snobs. And Alexis despised them – *them and every strand of their stringy, blonde hair.*

Already, Alexis (seething in her reverie) is enemy-centered toward a stranger whose name she doesn't even know until the smiling woman approaches the Crawfords to introduce herself. Her name is Blair. Of course, her name would be *Blair*. Alexis should've known her name would be something like *Blair*. However, despite her name, this woman, Blair, seems nice. She's nothing like those snotty brats from Alexis's high school and college years. And with that, Alexis backhands the salty chip off her shoulder and lets her guard down.

It may not be so bad after all. Alexis might love living in River Forest. And they all might become great friends and neighbors, Alexis, Sam, and these two perfect people, dubbed "TeddyBlair" by their closest associates.

But when it seems too good to be true, trust that more than likely it is. There is no such thing as perfection; Old Scratch knows that. But his job is to deceive human beings into believing otherwise; his modus operandi is to tempt human beings with sugary-sweet lies.

ROMANTIC RIVERS: AN ACT OF VOYEURISM.

The postpartum blues are all over Alexis Crawford, like a cheap suit, two weeks after the birth of her second child, a daughter she and Sam named Carter. But Sam is always away from home these days, with an excuse of working overtime to get that promotion to partner status at his firm. He's also (a lot) more aggressive and mentally abusive toward his once-mighty wife. Every chance the tall red-haired Sam gets to remind Alexis of just how much she's let herself go (since having children), he jumps at it. A jackass and then some, the snide and malicious Sam only seems to feel better when Alexis feels humiliated and lesser. Perhaps it would have been better if Alexis had gone after a partnership at her firm. Maybe then Sam, who has suddenly taken to referring to Alexis as an "old lady," to put in some overtime on her already fragile self-esteem, would be more loving and supportive. Perhaps then he would have something to boast about. Sam Crawford is an awful excuse for a husband; that much is true. But Teddy Bard? Teddy Bard has it all. He's the kind of man any woman would love to have for a husband—which is why Alexis couldn't help but feel envious when she caught a late-night glimpse of Blair "feeding" Teddy on one of the better couple's expensive sofas. Blair's golden head hung back, a look of otherworldly ecstasy on her flawless face, immersed in the passion of sensual oral pleasure. Alexis can only imagine the feeling because Sam hasn't made her feel that good in ages. She and Sam have not been intimate in months—and months; poor, pitiable Alexis.

Watching the erotic scene, her mouth agape, Alexis takes it all in, no pun. But what Alexis doesn't know is that this would be the last time she'd see Teddy Bard alive.

It will also mark the beginning of the end of her monotonous existence.

DOWN BY THE RIVERSIDE: THE MURDER OF TEDDY BARD.

The morning sun and misty dew of early autumn pair excellently in the limiting confines of the tony River Forest: another day, another peachy-keen day. Alexis is busy with typical activities involving her emotionally abusive husband and small children when she hears the whir of helicopter blades and the wail of police sirens. Something unpleasant has befallen their ritzy little cul-de-sac, but what could it be? What it could be is a body—discovered by a fisherman along the banks of the Potomac River. The corpse, brutally battered, with its skull crushed in several places, lay on the rocks beneath the trail. No one saw anything, so they all say, but authorities have identified the dead man as Teddy Bard.

For some (including Alexis), news of Teddy's remorseless murder comes as a jolting shock, but for others, not so much. The inhumanity of his death, right out in the open, speaks volumes. Who would want to kill such a nice man like Teddy? What damaging information did Teddy have in his arsenal? And against whom did he plan to use it? Who wanted their secrets to remain unknown? Who hated Teddy enough to crush his skull to dust? Behind their white-washed tombs, disguised as prime real estate, which of the wealthy River Foresters can sleep at night—knowing they committed a heinous murder?

And who set it in motion?

BEND OF THE RIVER: INTRODUCING THE NEIGHBORS.

As the narrative changes course to turn its glaring spotlight on the other residents of River Forest, Old Scratch breaks forth to gather up his obliging bondservants and shove them in it. As it happens, they number quite a few. Meet them as follows:

- Jennifer looks like a pin-up girl reminiscent of *Love, Jackie!* With luscious curves in all the right places and a doll-like face to match, many, including Alexis, wonder what the striking brunette sees in her tall, blubbery, sloppy, hot-headed, jealous, possessive, miserable, and unhandsome husband, Jeff. Perhaps it could be his money, as Jeff is nothing if not filthy rich.

Filthy-rich and scorned. Jeff has his trophy wife, but every other man (including those claiming to be so happily married to their respective wives) in the cul-de-sac wants her, too, his precious and beautiful Jennifer. It's too bad she won't stop enticing the fellas with her bouncy, bountiful bosom and big, round ass.

- Brash, big-boned, and Brazilian is the backstabbing, underhanded, two-faced, and ultra-horny alpha female named Laura. The 51-year-old vamp and her shady husband, Shawn, are the founders of a highly profitable security company—that Teddy wanted to snatch out from under them, much to their dismay—with agents stationed worldwide. But the dubious couple, especially Shawn, makes Alexis nervous; she thinks there is something suspicious about the former military man turned soccer coach. Why is Shawn always out in the woods, near the Crawford house, stalking the wee hours, claiming to be searching for his missing drones? Why is Shawn even operating drones in the neighborhood in the first place? And what nefarious activities have his little drones been recording? Did those drones record the killing of Teddy Bard? Are Shawn and Laura concealing information that may be vital to the murder investigation?

No one can out-slick a slickster. And while Shawn doesn't know it, the dark woods have eyes. Someone is always watching. And that someone knows something Shawn and Laura don't. On the contrary, Shawn and Laura know something THEY don't.

- They might be new to money, but Silicon Valley tech company founders Emily and Dylan are worthy of River Forest, regardless of what that self-important elitist, Blair, thinks. Emily, the genius coder, is a mousy, annoying, unsophisticated, relatively unattractive, arrogant, famous-name-dropping heifer; and Dylan, the conceited half-Pakistani man-whore, is one adulterous affair away from an incurable venereal disease, an unspeakable death—or both. Dylan likes to screw around, and Emily *knows* this; nevertheless, she stays married to him, preferring to blame the other women rather than her philandering, vulva-chasing husband. Emily is a dishrag and a doormat; she has no class, and her self-esteem is bottomless. But that fancy Blair? *She's* so confident that it makes Emily sick. *Blair* is the ultimate woman; she's everything the formerly poor Emily isn't. And Emily is envious, jealous, covetous—and enraged. Emily wholeheartedly believes that Dylan and Blair are carrying on (an affair) behind her back. And she sets out to prove it. She even uses a staged lunch date to recruit an unwilling ally to act as a second pair of eyes: her fellow doormat, Alexis.

Since Alexis and Blair are getting so tight, and she's always got her kinky-haired head all up Blair's anal canal, why not use her frumpy, needy ass? Ol' gullible Alexis will do anything to fit in—and feel accepted. Why, she'll do ANYTHING at all.

- Old man Mack likes them young; Mack likes them helpless. Old man Mack enjoys domination while engaged in copulation. Old man Mack is powerful, dangerous, and minted; Mack will pulverize any man (or woman) who dares to cross him. As he has done before, so will he do again—all one has to do is give him a reason. Mack can be a terrifying adversary, a man without mercy. And everyone in River Forest knows it. The old geezer gets what he wants when he wants it—or else. Old Mack will make one's blood run cold. And if he singles someone out, it will never end well. His eyes are beady, greedy, and lustful. And they are now roving the body of Alexis Crawford, the new neighbor. She looks ripe; she seems lost. She looks lonely; she seems sultry. She's quiet. She's defenseless. She's exotic. She's *Black*.

Mmm, wouldn't she be a delight, this forbidden fruit? When he approached her, she looked nervous. Was it the scars liver spots? Mack can only wonder. He'll have her, though—just like he's had all the others. Mack owns nearly all of River Forest. He can have take whatever (and whoever) the hell he wants. And he now wants the dark-skinned lady, Alexis.

RUSHING RIVERS: CHAOS IN THE COMMUNITY.

These all populate the cul-de-sac of great wealth and influence. And each one harbors a dangerous secret capable of destroying the others. Attempting to keep herself busy while Sam is away, yet again (and now that he's made partner at his firm, he has more excuses to spend as much time away from Alexis and their children as possible), Alexis has taken to a new hobby: gardening. And she's become quite good at it. Weeds have joined her growing list of enemies. And it's not until her pruning saw goes missing that Alexis realizes something is off.

What Alexis has been too blind to see, however, is that someone in her orbit hates her—with a passion—and wants her as dead as Teddy. Her greatest nemesis is the one she never would have imagined. Oh, how the foe hates.

POLLUTED RIVERBED(S): BEWARE THE ADULTERESS.

One woman could ask, Have you seen my husband? Another woman could say, I know you're having an affair with my husband! Followed by another woman who could say, I'll have your husband in as many ways as I want him; he'll do whatever I ~~ask~~ tell him to do. And then some other woman could demand, Stay away from my husband, you lying, whorish bitch!

But there is a forbidden woman who is like the harlot foretold in wisdom. She sits at the door of her house, calling out to the men who pass by, who go straight on their way. She entices the simple man with the sweetness of stolen water and the pleasantries of secretly eaten bread. She lures the simple man with the lie of her husband being away on a long journey, and with much seductive speech, she invites him into her bed, perfumed with myrrh, aloe, and cinnamon. But the Reaper is already there. And the hard object tenting her sheet is not the erection of a man—but a scythe.

The men of River Forest—despite their sickening machismo—are the simple ones who lack understanding. Misguided by carnal lust, they miss it and turn aside to her ways, straying into her path. These are those who lack sense, not understanding that the men who enter her house are already dead.

MUDDY RIVERS: DIRTY ROTTEN SCOUNDRELS.

Conniving, deceptive, hypocritical, cunning, adulterous, callous, malicious, jealous-hearted, passive-aggressive, sleazy, whorish, *self-hating*, vindictive, scandalous, vile, and incestuous are the Housewives of River Forest. And Andy Cohen himself wouldn't be able to clip muzzles on these rabid bitches. No one can stop a dog from returning to lap up its vomit, and no matter how often the sow has a bath, even still, she will return to wallowing in the mire.

RIVERS OF COLD BLOOD.

It's been six weeks since Teddy's murder, and the investigating detectives still have no leads in the case. Alexis is the only person who seems to care about what happened to Teddy, and Alexis Crawford is nothing if not tenacious. She is determined to learn the truth about who killed Teddy Bard and why.

But can she handle the truth and all its double-edged, albeit liberating, mercilessness? Or will lies, perverse and depraved as they are, be better to digest? Alexis means well, but pointing out the plank in the eye of another before first extracting the splinter from her own might prove fatal. Here, Alexis is sure she can swing it—until she runs face-first into the iron fist and smack-dab into a second (brutal) murder, the killing of another River Forest husband.

THE RIVER SUMMARY.

Narrated in the dual viewpoints of kindred spirits Alexis Crawford and Blair Bard—two women who will form a somewhat co-dependent bond—*What the Neighbors Saw*, co-starring Beryl Edwards as Blair's mean-spirited and bitter mother and Detectives Rich Bryan and Thomas Kim, two investigators around whom the residents of River Forest unbelievably continue to run rings, is a relatively well-written pincer grasp on the psyche; a composition of short, choppy chapters that read fast and ooze intrigue.

It is not until her plot on these pages nears its end that Melissa Adelman pushes down the plunger of her detonator to ignite a thunderous boom, blowing apart the mystery of the violent murder of Teddy Bard and the elaborate conspiracy that led up to it. Some readers might find this strategy annoying, but with this tale, Adelman will command forgiveness as her debut thriller boldly defends her honor, revealing intrinsic character development and flawless dialogue.

Adelman's strengths as a storyteller reveal themselves in the pros of her (literary) script. On the other hand, however, her weaknesses, minor as they might be here, are exposed in the cons, whereas the author left too many holes open in her haste to (finally) end it. Adelman was on a roll until her storyline became too bloated. There was some extra fat the plot could have done without, sure, but still, I understood Adelman's vision, and I must commend her for a job well done, even if a few blemishes caused the effort to fall short of a five-star review from me.

I do not possess the ability of a psychic, but if I had to guess, I would say that Melissa Adelman has what it takes to only get better with each succeeding effort, given she learns from her *limited* number of mistakes with this work.

My initial introduction to *What the Neighbors Saw* was with *The Minotaur Sampler, Vol. 8* (Macmillan Publishers, 2023), and I enjoyed the selection; I looked forward to completing the title. And so I have, and here we are. Melissa Adelman earned a new fan in me with this particular effort—of which she should be very proud—and I eagerly await her next release. Dear reader, I don't just recommend *What the*

Neighbors Saw; I highly recommend the title, especially if you like your mystery thrillers gritty, dramatic, action-packed, and unpredictable.

Happy reading, all.

REVIEWER'S NOTE: It is a pleasure to thank St. Martin's Press, Minotaur Books, and Macmillan Publishers—in association with NetGalley—for the complimentary copy of *What the Neighbors Saw* for my reading pleasure.

Analysis of *What the Neighbors Saw* by Melissa Adelman is courtesy of Literary Criticism by Cat Ellington for The Arts©.

DISCLOSURE: The "Callous Poem" included in my analysis of *What the Neighbors Saw* is an original piece created (by me) only for dramatic effect and to serve as a portion of my review.

Chapter Five

Unmasking Deformed Faces

*R*evenge is an eye for an evil eye;

"The Monsters Are Due on Alton Road"

The preceding Tanka of The Block Party

When their lips whisper,
their tongues wag, coated with mold,
and mildew and rash.
Then the drunkards, and their like,
come out to mangle and maul.

Analysis

Cat Ellington's Critique of *The Block Party*

Book by Jamie Day
(St. Martin's Press, 2023)

INTRODUCING ALEXANDRA FOX.

In yet another wealthy American suburban cul-de-sac, this time in a too-close-for-comfort little community on Alton Road, situated in the fictional setting of Meadowbrook, Massachusetts, we follow the storyline to a neighborhood Memorial Day block party in full swing. The music is thumping; the neighborhood kids are having fun—playing and squealing with delight; the tiki bar is open for business, and the neighborhood dads are all busy tending the grills. The Alton Road block party is an annual affair, and there has *never* been a dull moment in its history. By the way, the person responsible for organizing the yearly festivities is the queen bee of the coveted Altonites, our leading lady, Alexandra "Alex" Fox. Alex is a wife, mother, family lawyer turned divorce mediator, and "recovering" alcoholic.

From where we sit, observing the goings-on in the lives of this cast of characters, Alexandra is the first to take center stage. She moves about the block party, playing her part, smiling on the surface but grimacing within. While Alex has become a pro at putting on airs—feigning happiness—her home life is anything but joyous. She drinks (too much, too often) for the same reason most alcoholics do: to forget and numb the pain, if only briefly.

Alex and her husband, Nick, constantly bicker, and she has lost control of her only child, a teenage daughter named Lettie. Now the block party is on, and Alex is tipsy-tipsy. She's doing her best to avoid her husband, but he advances on her anyway, condemning her intoxication and ordering her to go home and sleep it off, which she does. A good nap can always chase away the drunk, but it's not so good at staving off the hangover. When Alex awakes, her head is pounding, and her mouth is bone-dry. And rather than hearing the smooth sounds of fireworks, music, and laughter from her neighbors enjoying the last remnants of their Memorial Day block party, Alex startles awake to the wailing sound of police sirens.

Dear reader, the stage is now set for a vicious, year-long chain of events that will make you question everything you thought you knew about the nature of humankind, everything you thought you knew about your friends, neighbors, and even your significant other. For here, the love—or lack thereof—of many will all but turn a cold shoulder and emote a bitter scowl.

Dear reader? Shall we recommence?

One Year Earlier

DEAR ~~ABBY~~ ALEX.

There are two things Alex Fox should have but doesn't: a clergy collar and a confession booth. Alex is the person everyone turns to for advice on how they should live, how to build better foundations for their marriages, what they should do about money issues, what to do if their spouse is cheating, how to handle domestic situations, what to wear and how to wear it, how they should bathe and brush their teeth and wash their hair, etc., etc., etc. People seek out Alex to tell her all their problems – and Alex, the confessor, is only too willing to advise, too intent on fixing their lives.

Perhaps the worst of those needing guidance is Alex's younger sister, Emily Adair, an unhinged, albeit highly in-demand real estate agent. The wife of Ken Adair, a successful software salesman (say that three times fast), the brunette, hazel-eyed Emily is jealous of her husband, Ken, and feels threatened by other (more beautiful) women. Ken had ONE affair before—or so he admits—and Emily has NEVER forgotten it. A realtor whose motto is the "Thrill of the Deal," Emily is always on edge, with one eye on the commissions and the other on her arrogant philanderer of a husband. Ken Adair is a dog; there's no doubt about it. Emily doesn't trust him, and in no uncertain terms does she let everyone in her miserable and insecure orbit know it. She'll be damned if she allows him to humiliate her again. And no matter what, her big sister, Alex, will always be in her corner. Emily can count on it.

One thing Emily didn't count on, however, was the arrival of a beautiful woman named Mandy Kumar—at whom the roving Ken has been making goo-goo eyes.

ON WEDNESDAYS, THEY WEAR PINK: THE MEAN GIRLS OF MEADOWBROOK MIDDLE SCHOOL.

Lettie Fox, the only lonely child of Nick and Alex, is not without her pubescent struggles. Smart as a whip, Lettie, an activist, is on the climate crisis committee at Meadowbrook Middle School, studying global warming, among other atmospheric ills that threaten the climatic health of planet Earth. Once a happy and carefree teen (with a dream of attending USC, never mind her dad's sternly advising UMass), Lettie is now withdrawn and antisocial—not to mention a social pariah and outcast. Lettie used to have friends, but that was before she fell victim to a small (and small-minded) group of mean girls led by her former best friend from childhood, the rich and snobbish Riley Thompson. A tramp in disguise, the blonde-haired Riley is the essence of popularity and the former president of the student council who struts about with the air of an A-list celebrity. Riley ("Rye," as her former friend turned foe, Lettie, likes to call her) knows there is a difference between right and wrong, but she prefers to do the latter. Riley and her arrogant posse (of girlfriends) delight in the evil they do to Lettie. The mean girls show no mercy, even dubbing the target of their oppressive treatment "Loony Lettie." What makes matters worse is that Riley is dating Lettie's cousin, Dylan Adair. *That*, on top of her hateful treatment of Lettie—which stings with the power of a scorpion.

The BMW-driving Riley Thompson is a liar, a backstabber, a betrayer, and a baby snake the world would be better off without. And Lettie would love to take her vengeance on the mean girl—if only she had the guts to do so. Lettie may have a little compassion left over in her broken heart, but not everyone shares her empathy. Riley Thompson—wearing her pink, expensive sneakers and snapping selfies on her pink, expensive phone—is a self-loathing skank.

She must pay, and she will—in the worst way possible.

THE BOY WITH THE SCORPION TATTOO.

On the day the Kumar family moves into the big, beautiful, expensive, and empty home on Alton Road, the festivities of the block party are already ongoing. Punjab, India native Samir, the controlling and jealous husband, is a psychiatrist; his lovely, tall, and blonde wife, Mandy, is a psychologist; and their good-looking (teenage) son Jay, the vaping boy with a scorpion tattoo on his wrist, is an aspiring hacker and a shady character for whom Lettie falls head-over-heels at first sight. Jay is the oldest surviving child of the distant Samir and Mandy, who lost their youngest boy, Asher, to a drowning death only a few years before. The weight of the untimely demise of her youngest child has taken an extreme toll on Mandy Kumar, but deep, dark secrets about her past are even more haunting.
Deep, dark secrets that now call Alton Road home.

Jay loves his mother and wants to protect her. And he will; he will defend her honor. He'll get the person who robbed his mother of her dignity and left her a broken woman.
Jay Kumar possesses a ruthless sting, the scorpion tattoo on his wrist betraying the true spirit of his nature. Unfortunately for Lettie, hell-bent on exacting revenge on mean girl Riley,

she will find this out the hard way. Jay knows something about Riley that Lettie doesn't. And the sickening secret is sure to crush her.

Jay Kumar knows the true identity of the Umbrella Man – the much older (and confidential) lover of Riley Thompson.

CREEPING ON THE DOWN-LOW: THE LUSTFUL NATURE OF KEN ADAIR.

Ken Adair is onery, full of himself. He was the big, popular jock in high school, the big man on his college campus, Ken Adair; he makes women swoon, Ken Adair; he can charm a woman straight out of her panties, *Ken Adair*. And his whiny, whimpering wife, Emily, should thank the gods that he found her worthy to be called his wife.

Ken Adair prides himself on the fact that only his genitalia can rival his ego in size. He's a boaster who purposefully engages in partiality towards his two sons, Logan and Dylan, favoring the elder Lacrosse champion Logan—who's more like his dear old dad, Ken—over the youngest, Dylan, who can't seem to live up to dad Ken's lofty standards. And none of it is doing the kid's mental health any good. While Dylan mopes around depressed and feeling like a failure, no thanks to his idiotic father, Ken, Death holds out its hand, pleading with Dylan that the young man would be better off in the netherworld of its realm. Given the atmosphere in the Adair household is already tense, no thanks to Ken's browbeating Dylan and his extramarital affairs for which Emily never (truly) forgave him, Ken Adair was just spotted by his sister-in-law, the nosy Alex, sneaking out the back door of the Kumars' new home and creeping into the woods beyond. No one but Mandy had been home at the time. So what was Ken doing there with her—alone? And what made Ken withdraw $25,000.00 from Emily's and his checking account? He claimed the suspiciously large withdrawal was for taxes—but was it? Ken and Emily have plenty of money (or so Emily says), but still. A quarter of one hundred thousand dollars is a lot of money—with the ability to raise red flags. Emily's missing emerald necklace is also cause for concern. Where is it?

Who took it?

PICTURE PERFECT — OR SO THEY APPEAR TO BE.

Willow Thompson is a tall and svelte thirty-something blonde who is awfully immaculate and always dressed to impress—for a woman with no job. How does she do it? How does Willow manage to stay so blemish-free, fat-free, and stress-free? Well, it doesn't take much effort when you're married to the world-famous fashion photographer Evan Thompson, a spoiled, arrogant jerk who fancies lording his money, or, rather, his family's money over others.

On the surface, the notable—and extremely temperamental—Evan Thompson, his beautiful wife Willow, and their pretty daughter Riley are the picture of perfection, a family with money and everything else for which the heart could wish. But the goings-on behind closed doors are disgusting and ugly things that have become adept at hiding themselves from the prying eyes of those fellow Altonites.

In the case of Evan and Willow Thompson, the phrase *opposites attract* is non-applicable. Willow hates the man and is desperate to divorce him, but she won't file the divorce papers for fear that Evan will leave her and Riley penniless. At least that's the story she tells her makeshift marriage counselor, Alex. But is that the whole truth? Or does Willow fear the level of fury Evan will unleash no sooner than he learns his precious little Riley is not his biological child?

Why, oh why, did she sign that stupid friggin' prenup for that … that bastard?!

OH, BROOKE, HOW THIS ONE MAN DESIRES THEE.

There is always one sex kitten who stands out among old maids. And the one on Alton Road is named Brooke Bailey. The ever-chic, gorgeous, worldly, sophisticated, and olive-skinned Brooke is a head-turner for days and days, possessing a body and face women envy and men desire. Brooke Bailey is courteous and genuinely kind, but still. Her smile lights up a room, and she seems to have no flaws—at least none Alex and Emily can see. Some, especially Alex, wonder what Brooke does for work, as they never see her leaving her opulent house on her way to any job, nor has Brooke ever shared details of her employment. There are many things the Altonites don't know about their attractive neighbor, Brooke, but one thing they do know is that she is the epitome of a woman who has it all, including a sexy, come-hither photo of herself on Nick's phone.

What the—? That should sober Alex up rather quickly.

Brooke Bailey is also a woman whose neighbors are suspicious about the death of her husband, Jerry. What happened to Jerry on that luxury cruise ship? Many in their community, particularly the judgmental females, suspect his fall overboard was no accident. And these would include Lettie, who thinks Brooke Bailey is a cunning, albeit stunning, femme fatale, although some men would beg to differ. The fellas on Alton Road may pretend they don't see her, but no one can deny the beauty of the former ~~stripper~~ exotic dancer, Brooke, not even Ken Adair, the former best friend—and partner in all manner of extreme indulgence—of the late Jerry Bailey. Her body is like fluid, the way it moves. It's like poetry in motion, one might say. And the man who will become her stalker would agree. He's the man who will send Brooke dirty, lovesick letters, confessing his devotion to her—and *only* her. He's the man who will kill to protect his filthy little obsession with Brooke.

His wife can never know.

PEST CONTROL.

The Bug Man is a pest exterminator with many enemies on Alton Road. Ken Adair and Evan Thompson just so happen to be two of his worst. These men hate the Bug Man, and they hate his aggressive sales tactics. They hate his cockiness and his annoying personality. But Bug Man couldn't care less; he takes a perverse pleasure in annoying the rich pricks. Ken and Evan want the Bug Man gone, and they will do whatever it takes to get him and his unwanted services away from them and their pristine little community.

Evan threatens to beat the Bug Man to a pulp, but Ken does one better. Ken moves heaven and Earth to get the pesty imbecile fired. So there. Power play. That'll teach the irritating bum to stay in his place!

Now that's done, they can all return to doing what they do best: evil.

One Year Later

Over an entire year, the stars of this striking tale become interwoven in a germ-infested cesspool brimming with the waste matter of hatred, revenge, alcoholism, drug abuse, adultery, jealousy, envy, covetousness, revenge, spite, rage, anger, rape, bullying, mental health woes, depression, hopelessness, broken spirits, domestic abuse, lies, malice, and vindictiveness. It all gets to be too much for our starring cast members. And before the annual Memorial Day block party comes to an end, two of them will be dead and gone – murdered in ice-cold blood.

Indeed, the human condition on Alton Road is gloomy, dark, and wickedly wrathful.

And none can attest to this better than the envious fault-finders who live outside the well-to-do confines of the Altonites, the same disapproving men and women who spend their entire days gossiping about their better-offs in a flimsy blog thread on the so-called Meadowbrook Online Community Page.

But even they should watch what they hate, lest they become it.

MY SUMMATION.

There is no gift in the world quite like that of storytelling. The ability to tell a story with detail to plot, a distinction of character development, and a singular style in the craft of writing are all the features that make an author exceptional. And if *The Block Party*, the debut novel of Jamie Day, is any indication of her capacity, I can hardly wait to read her follow-up effort, *One Big Happy Family*. Jamie Day, indeed, shows herself approved here. Phenomenal writing—and a witty way with words! Jamie Day put her foot in this one!
Whenever I feel compelled to re-read dialogue in a book because the writing is that darn good, that's saying something.

Co-starring Grady O'Brien as a young officer tasked with the misfortune of investigating the troubled lives of the Altonites and Monique LaSalle, who plays her bit part well as a close relative of Riley's biological father (or bio-dad), *The Block Party*, narrated in the dual viewpoints of Alex and Lettie (the latter an Aries character I will love forever), is a home run hitter, an outstanding tale; mysterious, heartfelt, emotional, and meaningful—not to forget thrilling, twisty, and remarkably suspenseful.

I do believe that many readers will thank God they're alive after reading *The Block Party*. The same will want to grab their loved ones and hug them, kiss them, and appreciate them all the more.

Concluding this tale, I couldn't turn the pages fast enough as I sat glued to the proverbial edge of my seat. Notwithstanding a pinch of typos typical of an unedited gallery proof, *The Block Party* rendered such a fascinating read that those few flaws were easily forgivable. I enjoyed this neatly-compacted narrative, dear reader, and I am sure you will share my sentiments. Consider it highly recommended.

Five block-party-pooped stars.

REVIEWER'S NOTE: I am pleased to thank St. Martin's Press for the complimentary copy of *The Block Party*—via NetGalley—for my reading pleasure.

Analysis of *The Block Party* by Jamie Day is courtesy of Literary Criticism by Cat Ellington for The Arts©.

"The Ultimate Finality"

The preceding Tanka of *Gone Tonight*

*A worm never dies
within the dead in the pit,
as the soul lies still.
And with it, a scorching flame,
that no cool water quenches.*

Analysis

Cat Ellington's Critique of *Gone Tonight*

Book by Sarah Pekkanen
(St. Martin's Press, 2023)

My Opening Statement

I once read a quote of truism that I never forgot. It appeared in a little book with other inspirational quotes that I found particularly commanding. It was the following:

"A conscience is God's built-in warning system. Be very happy when it hurts you. Be very worried when it doesn't."

I discovered that quote in the summer of 1994. And while it is still unknown to me who uttered those words, I remain, even to this day, in complete awe of them. Indeed, the human conscience *is* a powerful moral sense. And while many people fall into the category of the former—the ones who heed their conscience and seek to better themselves through the second chance of forgiveness—many more account for the latter, those who, for sport, do evil without fear of divine retribution. And their end is consistently the same: destruction and death—followed closely by Hades.

The characters who star in the (suspenseful) psychological thriller currently under review will serve as prime examples of individuals in those two groups representing both parts of a whole.

Dear reader? Shall we proceed?

You and Me Against the World

If the classic 1974 song, "You and Me Against the World," written by the legendary songwriting team of (Kenny) Ascher and (Paul) Williams—and recorded by the equally eminent Helen Reddy—could be the soundtrack for this intriguing work of fiction, it would fit our co-leading ladies, 42-year-old Ruth Sterling and her 24-year-old daughter Catherine to a T!

It would in the beginning, at least.

For twenty-four years, nothing in the world mattered to Ruth but Catherine. She and her only child were all Ruth cared about. And Ruth Sterling had a duty to protect them both—no matter what. Ruth Sterling, a desperate and distinctively troubled woman, risks life and limb to keep her dearest Catherine under her watchful eye—at all times, except for when the two women have to work their jobs. Even then, Ruth always knows Catherine's whereabouts, as the two Sterling women share the same phone plan with location access (for tracking purposes).
Ruth and Catherine are akin to "Lorelai Gilmore" and "Rory Gilmore"; the two women do everything together. They eat,

sleep, and breathe one another. Additionally, they also share an email address and an Amazon account. And though they are members of the working-poor class, *they survive together* – no outsiders necessary. When one of them gets ill, the other gets ill. It's that simple. Ruth and Catherine Sterling are mother and daughter. And they jointly possess an unbreakable bond. Catherine is so attached to her mother that Ruth knows how emotionally crippling it will be for Catherine to learn that Ruth is in the early stages of the debilitating brain disorder, Alzheimer's disease.

Oh, how emotionally crippling it will be.

The Dance of Deception Begins

- *Catherine*

A tall, golden-haired beauty, Catherine is working toward her nursing degree specializing in geriatric medicine. She is employed part-time at the one-hundred-thousand-dollar-a-year assisted living facility, Sunrise Senior Living, and plans on moving to Baltimore, where she will attend the Johns Hopkins Hospital to prepare for a rewarding career in health care. Catherine has always focused on her professional aspirations, but now her attentiveness has shifted gears. Her beloved mother—and best friend—Ruth is sick, suffering from the early onset symptoms of Alzheimer's, an unfortunate hereditary condition, according to Ruth, whose own barbarous mother allegedly succumbed to the vicious effects of senile dementia.

Catherine knows—all too well from her patients on the Memory Wing at Sunrise Senior Living—the symptoms of her mother's cerebral defects and how significant those conditions are. And she will do whatever she can to care for her mother, even if it means putting her own life (and dreams) on hold. Baltimore can wait. The cable-ready apartment Catherine had lined up and ready to be lived in can wait. The Johns Hopkins Hospital, a gateway to a much (*much*) better life for Catherine, can wait. It can ALL wait! Her ailing mother needs her now more than ever. The younger Sterling woman can only feel her heart breaking in bits and pieces as she watches Ruth searching for her misplaced keys, storing eggs in the cabinet rather than the refrigerator, and referring to ice cubes as "water cubes." It's all too overwhelming for Catherine; she's having too hard a time digesting Ruth's declining memory lapses emotionally. She is thirsty for answers concerning her mother, and a visit with neurologist Dr. Alan Chen is just what they both need. Ruth, although reluctantly, agrees to accompany Catherine to his office, and the communication between doctor and patient is going well until Dr. Chen insists that Ruth undergo a CT scan and lumbar puncture, together with a PET scan and MRI, to help him and his team better understand the root cause of her symptoms, which, according to Ruth, have been lingering for a while, much to Catherine's surprise.

Her mother never told her that.

The dumbfounded Catherine, frantic to save and prolong her mother's life, is enthusiastic about the idea of a CT scan, but

Ruth? Not so much. Ruth Sterling has no intention of laying still for any CT scans or lumbar punctures and creates a ton of excuses as to why she is so opposed to the procedures. Ruth—using her alleged family history of Alzheimer's as a justification for her disinterest—has no faith in any "miracle cure" that may stop, or at least slow down, the progression of her illness. And this also strikes Catherine as odd.

Why would her mother *not* want to move a mountain or two to better her health? And why is her mother not being more transparent about her family and past? What else is Ruth hiding? Hmm, good questions... Good questions, indeed.

Not only does the curious Catherine intend to find answers to those nagging questions, but she is determined to learn more about her mother's past life—and those who were part of it. But will Catherine be able to handle the unpleasant truth—about her mommy, Ruth?

- *Ruth*

Some people keep secrets, and some others keep *secrets*. And Ruth Mary Sterling is working hard to keep quite a few of those of emphasis from her darling daughter, Catherine. Ruth works as a waitress in a greasy-spoon diner just a city bus ride from where she and Catherine live in a humble two-bedroom apartment in Harrisburg, Pennsylvania. A former citizen of Lancaster, Pennsylvania, Ruth had to abandon her hometown in haste after her life crashed into a brick wall during her high school days.
It was a long time ago, but memories of her past still haunt Ruth, a woman on the run for twenty-four years. She barely

eats because she needs to be thinner than she once was. And though her hair was once glorious and lustrous and hung past her waist, the former Poms squad dancer had no choice but to cut it short – to look as average as possible. Put plainly, the present life Ruth Sterling lives is a lie. Ruth's driver's license is a fake; she can never utilize her given name or make her locality known in the system; she must remain under the radar and do everything in her power to protect Catherine. Ruth knows the truth. She stays abreast of her past in Lancaster and the people she once knew by searching for them on the Internet at her local library, stalking their social media feeds, and reading the local papers for any articles that might still mention her. Ruth reads the social media postings of her father and her beloved brother, Timmy. And then she searches for news about *him*, the only man she ever loved besides her father and brother, the one man she must *never* allow to find her and Catherine.

Ruth is a woman on the verge of having her mind completely obliterated by fear, worry, anxiety, and paranoia. Not Alzheimer's, but fear, worry, anxiety, and paranoia. Because you see, dear reader, Ruth Sterling has concocted a fantastical lie: Ruth made up the Alzheimer's disease tale to manipulate her only child, to keep Catherine right where she wants her. Ruth even studied a book about the mind-altering disease to study its symptoms and varied terminologies. That done, she went into character, selfishly playing her misleading role and picking apart the volatile emotions of an unsuspecting Catherine—who voluntarily bid a promising future in health care adieu all so that she could stay close to home and care for her sweet, poor, helpless, "ailing" mother.

On the other hand, Catherine doesn't know that her sweet, poor, helpless, and supposedly ailing mother, Ruth, is playing her like a master pianist seated at the artist's bench of a grand Steinway.

But is Ruth Sterling really that cruel, sadistic, and unconscionable? Or is there looming a more sinister threat to her precious Catherine?

Curiosity Just Might Kill You

- *Catherine*

Catherine is determined to come to a knowledge of the truth concerning Ruth, so she formulates a scheme to trick her mother into revealing more details about her past, going so far as to order a copy of *Tell Me Your Life Story, Mom*, a family tree journal from Amazon to set her plan in motion. Ruth is fully aware of the purchase (mother and daughter share an Amazon account, mind you) but says nothing; *she plays the game.* But what Ruth is *unaware* of is that Catherine, while snooping through her mother's personal effects, found Ruth's library card and intends to go sleuthing with it.

In time, the meddling Catherine will get the answers she didn't expect, setting her life on a savage collision course with mayhem.

- *Ruth*

Keeping up her lying charade, Ruth has to be careful to remain in character. She feels guilty about deceiving Catherine—and for that reason, Ruth started a journal for her daughter to biograph her troubled past that led up to the present day—but her fear is of greater significance than her nudging conscience. Ruth cannot afford to let her guard down again like she did when she and Catherine shared their favorite meal for dinner, lasagna pizza. Ruth was desperate to throw Catherine a bone and allowed herself to reveal too much. She has to be more careful when she visits the local library to do her Internet trolling. Ruth has to keep abreast of the goings-on of those left behind so long ago. She needs to stay one step ahead of the parole board set to decide whether or not he's ready to be released, freed from his twenty-five-year sentence.

He did time while Ruth ran and hid. Her hands are just as bloody as his. Ruth knows that. And should the parole board grant his request to be released, he's going to hunt her and Catherine down—like the natural predator he is—and murder them both in cold blood, like the cold blood in which her Poms squad coach, the perverted pedophile, Daniel Franklin, was murdered all those years ago. Ruth used to worship him. He was her first love. But now he is her enemy, this devilish man from her past who torments her present and threatens her future—especially now. These thoughts trouble her mind as Ruth sits in the cozy confines of a public library, reading the varied news articles online. According to published reports, James Bates won over the board at his parole hearing. He will soon be a free man. And just as Ruth has never forgotten him, James Bates has *never* forgotten his accomplice, Ruth. It's time to run again, and

Ruth must get to Catherine fast. But she's too late, as her nosy daughter is already running, unknowingly, in the opposite direction—straight into the arms of a ferocious and angry psychopath whom her mother, Ruth, has only ever referred to as the "sperm donor."

Indeed, twenty-five years is a *long time* for one to do *(hard) time* for a *heinous crime* it took two, not one, to commit.

The (Fatal) Family Reunion

IF LIFE GETS HARD TO UNDERSTAND, COME TO POPPA—
COME SEE YOUR POPPA.

Her eyes are a striking shade of pale blue—just like his. She's his daughter, the daughter he never knew. And he now has the advantage as he watches her from under his baseball cap. He knows who she is, thanks to Facebook. She's a beauty, and of that, he's proud. He's a proud poppa. His daughter is beautiful – but she's also gullible. He reads her well as he scans her from his table at the old hangout of his and her mother, Pizza Piazzo. Catherine. Nice name. She came to find out more about her fugitive mother, the same one who left him to take the fall for that murder all those years ago.

Ruth was late to meet him. He got caught, but she didn't. He served time, but Ruth didn't. Ruth never wrote; she never called; the bitch never sent flowers—she just split, took off, and left him behind to take the fall for it all. But now he's free. And the daughter that the man named James Bates never knew he had is seated only feet away from him. He's got her mother—the former Ava Morales—in his crosshairs. All he has to do is follow the grease fire. All James Bates has to do is play one more hand. Sunrise (the assisted living facility) never looked so good. Vengeance is his; he will repay; he will repay the woman who broke his arctic heart. James Bates has yet another sinister plan.

And with that, dear reader, the ill-fated family reunion between Mama, Poppa, and their little cub gets underway—leading to the long-awaited morbid death of one.

And here, we ask, Is there such a thing as the perfect murder? Who is the REAL monster? Who is the one unfazed by their seared human conscience? The one that can kill another human being so mercilessly and not bat an eye—just go about life as if all they did was swat a fly.

Introducing the Co-Stars

While Ruth, Catherine, and James Bates shine in their top-billing, those who co-star alongside them render performances just as memorable. They include the following:

- Mateo Morales plays his part as a kind, patient, and hard-working man given to the adoration of his two children, Ruth (née Ava Morales) and Timmy.

- Timmy Morales shines in his quiet role as Ruth's younger brother and the apple of her eye. Timmy's words are few, but his presence on these pages is voluminous.

- Brittany Davis—Ruth's former best friend turned worst enemy—is a cruel, lying witch, a typical mean girl, a-a-a-a-nasty stuck-up tramp, a skank, and a snobbish cheerleader, who real-life actress Allie DeBerry would play the crap out of were this a made-for-TV film.

- Melanie is a waitress and supposedly good friend of Ruth. Catherine and Melanie join forces to keep tabs on Ruth, but Ruth Sterling? Ruth Mary Sterling wasn't born yesterday.

- Tin is a wonderful—and understanding—woman and Catherine's supervisor at Sunrise Senior Living. While not too prominent in this fictional script, Tin still has a speaking role and plays her bit part well.

- Rosie is a special kind of rose, a beautiful soul on whom Ruth, her former Poms squad teammate, could always count, even during their high school years. And her role on these pages doesn't go without notice.

- Ethan, the tattooed vodkaholic and whorish bartender, co-stars as Catherine's first love and the rotten, worm-filled apple of Ruth's suspicious eye.

- George and June Campbell co-star in this tale as the delightful older couple who adore Catherine as if she's their granddaughter. The pair would do anything for Catherine within their means. But George and June—ol' gullible George and June—on account of Catherine, are about to fall prey to the rage of a fire-breathing dragon.

My Summation

Sarah Pekkanen's *Gone Tonight* is a clutching psychological thriller overflowing with thrills, suspense, deception, humor, and warm sentiment.

Concerning the subject of Alzheimer's disease and its many debilitating factors, Pekkanen's research here is so thorough that she should be assigned an ORCID iD.
The author slam-dunks her plot on these pages, her pen brilliantly composing a tale of flawless rivet and shattering revelations.

Exposing an array of spiritual nemeses common to humans, from fear, worry, doubt, anxiety, and paranoia to emotional dependency, neediness, pride, lying and denying, hate, anger, and the inhuman murderous spirit, Pekkanen crafts her fast-paced, short-chaptered tale, narrated in the dual viewpoints of Ruth and Catherine, throughout three acts of edge-of-your-seat entertainment. And once again, she impressed me—with her silky-smooth writing style.

Of course, there are always cons, especially with uncorrected galley proofs that haven't completed the editing stage before publication. But with *Gone Tonight*, I encountered only a few minor typos that paled in comparison to Pekkanen's applaudable storytelling, her technique with character development, and her fascinating way with words. Aside from a blemish or two, I could see her vision. And I enjoyed it.

I laughed out loud and cried; I felt the heavy chill of suspense and cried some more. At one point, I had to remove my reading glasses to keep the teardrops off their lenses. I was genuinely intrigued by the storyline of *Gone Tonight*, although its conclusion felt slightly rushed.

Tales about the bonding between mothers and daughters—especially those taking on the difficult trials of life head-on while realizing they're all each other have in the face of a threat—tend to set me on an emotional roller-coaster. And this one was a real tear-jerker at times.

Sarah Pekkanen's latest effort, *Gone Tonight*, is a winner with me, which is unsurprising as I have yet to be disappointed with her gift of writing. It is a tale that I would go out of my way to recommend to fans of psychological thrillers that embody a dark soul and a sinister mind. Kudos, Ms. Pekkanen. You have done it again.

Five...homicidal stars.

REVIEWER'S NOTE: It is a pleasure to thank St. Martin's Press for the complimentary copy of *Gone Tonight*—via NetGalley—for my reading pleasure.

Analysis of *Gone Tonight* by Sarah Pekkanen is courtesy of Literary Criticism by Cat Ellington for The Arts©.

DISCLOSURE: The reference to the fictional characters "Lorelai Gilmore" and "Rory Gilmore" is from the Warner Bros. Television, Dorothy Parker Drank Here Productions, and Hofflund/Polone TV series "The Gilmore Girls" (2000-2007)

Chapter Six

Hoodwinking and False Impressions

*Y*es, *a tooth for a rotten, rancid tooth.*

"Metaphor"

The preceding Tanka of *Keep Your Friends Close*

It took a bird's wings,
and it flew far, far away,
leaving carnage in its wake.
Here today, gone tomorrow;
the brevity of one's life.

Analysis

Cat Ellington's Critique of *Keep Your Friends Close*

Book by Leah Konen
(Penguin Group Putnam / G.P. Putnam Sons, 2024)

"Those who oppress the poor insult their Maker, but those who are kind to the needy honor Him."
—Proverbs 14:31

The Prelude

THERE WILL BE BLOOD.

The woman, already a nervous wreck, enters the too-quiet home in pursuit of peace. It was all she ever wanted. Peace. A friendly greeting was to be the olive branch. Mutual respect. She had waited for so long on this day. Her voice, the one ignored for years, would finally be heard. And she was ready, ready to make amends. The paint, blood-red in hue, was the first thing she saw upon entering the home. She initially thought it was paint as the house was undergoing a renovation. It was everywhere, the "red paint." Smeared on the hardwood floors and some of the walls. She called his name, but there was no answer. As she ventured further into each room of the house, at last coming to the opening of the deluxe kitchen, she realized that the "red paint" wasn't paint at all but blood. And there he lay—drowned in a pool of it.

His gaping head wound betrayed his manner of death, and his gray eyes stared, unseeing. On the wall above his corpse—and in his blood—were the bitterly vindictive words spelled out: *DIE RICH PIG*

From there on, a detailed recounting of events will reveal how our leading lady's life became a puzzling maze of deception, envy, adultery, greed, hatred, lies, covetousness, idolatry, and eventual murder.

Dear reader? Shall we meet Mary Haywood?

Our starring lead, Mary Haywood, is a journalist who has been out of the loop of her profession for far too long and seeks to rekindle her passion for reporting. As the curtains open to showcase the fictional play in action, Mary is seated at the bar of an eatery in the wealthy New York State town of Woodstock, chatting with a nosy bartender and pondering over her next residence and a new daycare facility for her (nearly) two-year-old toddler, Alex. The divorce from her husband and the child's father, George, has thus far proven messy and vitriolic. And Mary is under a great deal of stress. George Haywood is playing games with his and Mary's child custody arrangements, using his immense wealth and the extended tentacles of his powerful family's connections to crush his soon-to-be ex-wife. But because she loves her little boy, Mary is determined to fight it out in court, although she fears her strenuous efforts will come to naught.

Of course, Mary was hesitant when George—heir to the Haywood real estate empire—offered her a rent-free property to live in with Alex in Woodstock while the soon-to-be exes worked out their parting arrangements, but for the sake of keeping the peace, she agreed. Mary is ready to move on with her life – as she should be. Her marriage to George Haywood, although privileged, was hellish at times. And a new start, hopefully with some nice alimony, is just what Mary needs. That, and a career refreshment.

Mary thinks about all this when she spots her from the window inside the bar. Her hair is a different color, but it's her. She's with a different man—and child—but it's her. Mary could spot that statuesque height, lithe body, and that perfect face from a million miles away. It's her. Willa.

What the hell is Willa—who hasn't called her in ages—doing in Woodstock? Mary wonders.

The First Stage (Past Tense)

THE WOMAN AT THE PLAYGROUND.

Mary Haywood is nothing if not a doting mother to her toddler son, Alex. And this had been obvious to the other well-heeled moms who watched over their little ones as the tots wore themselves out on a fun-filled day at that playground one year ago. That was the day Mary met her. She had been at the play area—in the sandbox—with a little boy she called Jack Junior. The woman was bold and self-confident, attributes Mary picked up on immediately. And she was *pretty*, the perceptively carefree woman was. She appeared so sweet, and she dared anyone to judge her for feeding her kid, not healthy options such as fresh-cut veggies and fruit but Lay's potato chips.

Her style was impeccable, as was her hair. And her nails and teeth were showstopping. The woman didn't look like she belonged in a kiddie park with the other (average) frumpy-and-lumpy mommies. No, she was a stand-out among all of them.

She had a toddler, too, but who could tell? Her body revealed no extra fat or loose skin, and her eyes defied the dark circles and puffiness that stemmed from a lack of sleep. Mary inhaled the woman's image and then exhaled her (own) self-loathing before the stranger—wearing an elegant sapphire necklace that accentuated her blue eyes perfectly, no less—finally spoke. Her name was Willa. No surprise there. With a name like Willa, she had to be a beauty – at least outwardly.

Willa initiated the conversation, and before long, she and Mary were chatting it up like lifelong friends. The two women bonded further as their tots played, and as fate would have it, Mary and Willa exchanged numbers and agreed to meet up (again) for lunch and drinks.

Mary Haywood might be breaking up with great wealth, but this woman, Willa, is still on the right arm of money—and she shows her new best friend, Mary, a good time all over (the gentrified) Brooklyn. At Willa's expense, the two new friends head out to Lincoln Center to enjoy a performance of

La bohème, followed by a nightcap at an upscale spot for more salty margaritas. Willa not only holds her (hard) liquor well, but she is also extremely curious, querying the tipsy—and needy—Mary about nearly every aspect of her life. At the same time, Willa reveals very little about herself – on purpose. Her job is to worm her way into Mary's good graces. And with time, she does just that.

Willa

Spawned from humble beginnings, where the only aroma she ever wore was the stench of poverty, Willa, née Charlotte Anne Williams, now revels in the material wealth and monetary riches hard-earned by others, particularly men. Nevertheless, her mindset is low-class and a vindictive reminder. Indeed, if it had a mouth with which to speak out loud, Willa's mindset would do so in a malicious tone of voice that would say to her, *You may be all dolled up and dressed to the nines now, but you're STILL a poor, scraggly, hand-to-mouth urchin.* And Willa would be damned if she proved it right.

Willa does, however, have an insatiable need to prove she's rich; therefore, she makes a show of flashing her American Express Black Card—or the *Centurion*, if you will—before the eyes of an emotionally grieved Mary to both impress her (with drinks, dinners, lunches, operas, and shopping trips) and win her over. So far, so good. It doesn't take Mary long to fall head over heels for her new best friend, Willa.

Take *THAT*, Cassandra! *Cassandra. My, how the mighty have fallen.*

The Second Stage (Present Tense)

Cassandra

Mary is not the only former Mrs. Haywood to fall off. Cassandra, the ex-wife of Henry, Mary's former brother-in-law, is also a present-day train wreck, no thanks to her spiteful, malicious, vindictive, and ruthless ex-husband. An angry and desperate Cassandra, like her former ally and closest friend, Mary, is falling into the abyss of poverty now that she no longer has access to a life of ease and the best ~~things~~ stuff money—and lots of it—can buy. Cassandra and Mary were once close and thick as thieves, but now Cass acts like she hates Mary, blaming Mary for everything miserable in the world, including divorce. Cassandra, a ravishing beauty, was always content to be the trophy for the philandering Henry. Cassandra was always content to look the other way—so as not to make direct eye contact with abuses of both the physical and mental nature. Cassandra had a promising career once but left it all behind for *Henry*. And now the bastard wants to destroy her. He took everything she needed to start over, including her precious jewels. Cassandra would have let the money go if she could have only kept her jewels—

Oh, those jewels; they would have taken her a long way.

NO luxury jewel house was out of Cassandra's reach in her married-to-a-Haywood day. She had only the finest pieces ever created, pieces even the late Liz Taylor would have marveled at – violet eyes transitioning to a bright shade of Kelly green with envy. The magnificent jewels gifted to Cassandra boasted fineries from the houses of Bvlgari, Harry Winston, Tiffany & Co., Chopard, Van Cleef & Arpels, and the numero uno of them all, the Charles Jacqueau designed Panthère de Cartier, a breathtaking diamond-and-gold bracelet produced by the Maison of Cartier.

Over five hundred thousand dollars in retail was the value of Cassandra's jewels. And just ONE piece would have set her up nicely on the path to a new life post-Henry Haywood. But he had to take it away from her—that nasty, vindictive, hateful, malicious bastard!

Someone should kill him. Someone should kill that ornery bastard as dead as he has to go.

The Third Stage (Past Tense)

~~FRIENDS~~ **ENEMIES WITH BENEFITS.**

Mary, Willa, and George

Mary can't stop thinking about Cassandra. The two women, who both hailed from impoverished families, married the wealthy and powerful Haywood brothers—George and Henry—and lived like royalty before their individual lives came crashing down. Now Cassandra is lost with nowhere to go and no money to get there, and Mary is only hanging on because of her and her soon-to-be ex-husband's only child, Alex. Here, the chubby-cheeked toddler, the pride of Mary's life, has become a tool, a weapon of sorts, for manipulation—to be used (against his mother) by not only the child's father but also his hostile grandparents and Uncle Henry.

George Haywood is just as brutal and baleful as his sibling Henry—although he pretends to be more passive—and nothing more than a control freak, a masochistic sadist, an arrogant prick, and an adulterer. Yes, a lying, filthy adulterer who eagerly ran over Mary's abdominal stretch marks and limp, stretched-out breasts—the result of breastfeeding Alex—to get to that tight, firm, youthful, curvy, and supple body belonging to Mary's so-called new best friend, Willa.

Willa has been sleeping with Mary's husband in Mary's bed, sweating and discharging genital fluids on Mary's thousand-thread-count sheets, feeding Mary's toddler Cheerios, and then eating and wiping her mouth and saying to herself, *I've done nothing wrong.* However, her (guilty) conscience begs to differ.

Regardless, Willa is on a mission. She's thinking about her future—because, after all, Jack Senior might say one day, "Get the hell out!" and then where will she be?

Survival trumped any emotional feelings of guilt when Willa chose to follow her gut instincts. Knowledge is power. And Willa picked Mary's liquor-impaired brain bare to obtain as much of it as possible. It took a while, but Mary soon revealed details about Cassandra's treasured jewels: *George has them. They're in a soft black velvet bag inside his and her bedroom's safe at the brownstone...* The intoxicated, bitter, and heartbroken Mary had finally confided.

Once she got the information she wanted, Willa was willing to risk her setup with cash cow Jack Senior and his spoiled mini-me, Jack Junior, by embarking on a dangerous affair with George Haywood to get her hands on the extraordinary wealth. Willa was also willing to do whatever it took to defend her dear Mary's remaining honor—as Willa's motto is this: "I'm the sort of person who would do *anything* for my friends."

But would the spirit of hatred—she secretly harbors towards the rich—instruct her to commit *murder*?

The Fourth Stage (Present Tense)

George and Henry

In 1986, (the legendary) Billy Joel sang a musical tale about the "Modern Woman," in which Bill informed the male subject of the tune that the chic woman of the man's dreams, who had her "own money," was not "another honey" a man like the subject could "quickly disarm," thereby an independent woman who earned her keep and had no need to become dependent on the economic means of any man. Indeed, financial independence has its advantages, and it is for this reason that controlling and abusive men like George and Henry Haywood have a preference for women, who, before (luckily) being courted by them, lived from hand to mouth in a rat race society, where the poor and working-class far outnumber the wealthy. The Haywood clan—New York's top real estate oligarchs—love to lord it over others. They *love* to do evil and then laugh in the faces of those they hurt: for the one who is to be taken captive, into captivity he shall go; and he who kills with the sword, in the same manner, will be destroyed. Unfortunately, proud, worldly people like the Haywoods don't think this way; they shun, spurn, and ignore sound wisdom and understanding. They maltreat and oppress – until they run into individuals worse than themselves.

Here, one of them will be met by another filled up with a blood-lustful vengeance – and deceased in a coppery-scented pool of cold blood will he lay.

A savage blow from a friend turned foe.

The Showdown

THOU SHALT ~~NOT~~ KILL.

The Haywoods are a family of privileged people who love to bring pain and suffering to those who already have it hard enough in life. They're the sort of people who know and believe that they can get away with anything, *anything at all.* They could destroy the career of one who rubbed them the wrong way or cause poverty to befall another by bulldozing that person's financial house off its foundation. Hell, the

Haywoods could even take someone's children away from them and dare that same someone to try challenging the spiteful move in any court of law. They are like eels on dry land, the Haywoods. And a certain someone *hates* them. A certain someone hates that wicked, godless, arrogant family—with only the most fierce passion; hence, the individual thinks, contemplating just how they will go for the kill. The person measures their time, and in the privacy of their mind, the individual plans the perfect murder of a Haywood heir. And no one would ever suspect them because no one knows they exist.

You have heard that it was said to the people long ago, 'You shall not murder, and anyone who murders will be subject to judgment.' But here, one individual *will* kill—in an unrelenting and unrepentant fit of white-hot rage.

Indeed, it will all come to a head with the crushing of a skull.

The Troubled (Supporting) Ensemble

Dear reader, a scandalous and vile script calls for an ensemble of scandalously vile characters. Such are those supporting and bit players who round out a well-performed cast on the pages of this mean-spirited—and morally offensive—tale. Joining our starring leads are none other than the following:

- Frank and Ruth Haywood are twin demons and the narcissistic parents of George and Henry. Ruth, the loudly aggressive one, and Frank, the quietly aggressive one, work as a unit to tear the soul of another to pieces without sympathy or empathy—as their nature is carnal, debased. But then again, wouldn't it take two monsters to raise two monsters?

- Jack Senior is the father of the toddler Jack Junior and the scorned former lover of the much younger Willa. A rich, handsome, and tanned silver fox, Jack Senior feigns anger and humiliation well, but is he a kind, older gentleman worthy of consolation, or is he a remarkable master of deceit?

- Rich is Willa's monotonous new lover and the father of a little girl named Poppy—another child for whom Willa will act as a makeshift mother. Rich, the wealthy owner of a beautiful farmhouse in Woodstock, seemingly means well, but on these pages, if he were software, he'd be bloatware.

- Detective Morales is the woman investigating the George Haywood murder case. And she is convinced she has the right suspect—until all the players start running rings around her, muddying up the linoleum floors of her headquarters.

My Summation

A storyline set in New York, from Brooklyn to Woodstock to Old Forge, *Keep Your Friends Close* is a genuinely entertaining read. Leah Konen, obviously inspired by the great Agatha Christie, does a fantastic job weaving her plot and developing her characters—some lovable, others repulsive—on these pages while folding in a healthy helping of mystery and intrigue and boggling the reader's mind with one unpredictable twist after another. And although the story, told over three parts, became slackened somewhat near the conclusion, making me wonder if it would ever end, Konen, to her credit, compensated for the shortcoming with a solid, action-packed—and at times emotional—chronicle.

Keep Your Friends Close touches on a generous deal of feminism and will undoubtedly hit a home run with the "girl power" set but might offend several others. Added, if the reader holds an eat-the-rich-because-life-is-a-bitch philosophy, this narrative is sure to prove quite satisfying. Leah Konen is a very talented writer; her effort here reveals that much. But near the end, I yawned once or twice—or thrice—and that was not a good thing. I was rooting for Konen to pick up the pace, and the author did just that: she caught her breath and got back in it, and her tale's minor blemishes, only a few on an otherwise lovely canvas, were forgiven. Yes, the plot taking a slow and draggy turn did induce fatigue in me, but Konen quickly refreshed its energy, guiding it to the finish line with grace, and for that, her narrative is worthy of an extra point.

To the mystery thriller enthusiast, *Keep Your Friends Close* is a forceful effort that I would recommend, and highly so, as I am sure the same will enjoy its "whodunit" premise. And because I find Leah Konen's writing style rather pleasing, I look forward to reading her 2022 release, *The Perfect Escape*, which I have a new copy of in my library of print books. For now, though, *Keep Your Friends Close* was admirably hard-won with me. The tale fought like hell. And it won.

Five wealth-corroding stars.

REVIEWER'S NOTE: Thank you to Penguin Group Putnam / G.P. Putnam Sons—in association with NetGalley—for the complimentary copy of *Keep Your Friends Close* for my reading pleasure.

Analysis of *Keep Your Friends Close* by Leah Konen is courtesy of Literary Criticism by Cat Ellington for The Arts©.

"A ~~Tale~~ Tell of Delusions"

The preceding Tanka of *The Influencer*

Democratized fame
feeds chum to the deluded,
and gives him false hope.
His madness is unrestrained;
his self-loathing, unabashed.

Analysis

Cat Ellington's Critique of *The Influencer*

Book by Miranda Rijks
(Inkubator Books, 2021)

```
The following analysis contains coarse
language that some readers might find
offensive. I would strongly advise viewer
discretion.
—Cat Ellington
```

The Launch "Pad"...

influencer
/ˈinflo͞oənsər/

noun

- **MARKETING**

a person with the ability to influence potential buyers of a product or service by promoting or recommending the items on social media.

Internet celebrity

An internet celebrity, also referred to as a social media personality or an influencer, is an individual who has acquired or developed their fame and notability on the Internet.
—Wikipedia

Famous for being famous

Famous for being famous, in popular culture terminology, refers to someone who attains celebrity status for no particular identifiable reason, or who achieves fame through association with a celebrity. The term is a pejorative, suggesting the target has no particular talents or abilities.
—Wikipedia

Legitimate fame—as opposed to Illegitimate fame

(I) "It is obvious that celebrities grow their reputation by standing out in one or more areas in the entertainment industry. These areas can generally be sports, cinema, music or television. The fame that celebrities gain is usually because they are successful and talented in their field."
— Sıla Ekşioğlu, *INFLOW*

(II) "Social media fame is more fragile and less likely to endure compared to the celebrity of actors and musicians."
—Fielding Graduate University

(III) "The fame you get through social media is as fake as your online friends. It means nothing in the real world unless you are famous in real life as well."
—Voice from *Quora*

Truth

"In the future, everyone will be famous for 15 minutes."
—Andy Warhol

"With the advent of reality TV and YouTube, average people everywhere receive their share of the spotlight."
—Pennsylvania Center for the Book - Penn State, in response to the famous Andy Warhol quote

"Everybody wants to be famous, but nobody wants to do the work."
—Kevin Hart

My Opening Statement...

The first time I saw the word "Influencer" on the Internet—as it related to members of the general public who are supposedly famous for either dancing in homemade videos or promoting off-brand products to their large numbers of followers on social media platforms—my first verbal reaction was, "What the hell is a damn social media

Influencer?" I had no idea, so I researched it. And I found the meaning of it offensive, just as I did with the so-called titles "Internet famous," "Instagram celebrities," "Twitter famous," "YouTube stars," "Web stars," "TikTok stars," "Going viral," and other terms/phrases/idioms of the like.

Nothing is more delusional than an everyday person "acquiring fame" without notable (public) works meriting it or as insulting as reputable journalists—associated with legitimate media organizations—giving credence to the madness. The latter loses all credibility (and respect), while the former never had any in the first place.

There is no truth, in my opinion, to the phrase "Famous for being famous"; an individual who has legitimately crossed the line of becoming famous must have noted public works for which they are known in their respective field or industry, be it entertainment (including music, movies, television, and sports), art (the humanities), sciences, literature, journalism, politics, fashion, or religion. Not on social media platforms dancing in homemade videos or showing off a make-believe lifestyle—for social likes. *That* is not legitimate fame, at least not in my opinion. But then again, I am shamelessly old-school, a member of Generation X, and unapologetically in favor of Baby Boomers and Gen X. I am the product of an era that accepted nothing less than the best. Either one had it (genuine talent), or they did not. There was no room for confusion; the fakers got called out for what they were.

Ordinary people who obtained short-lived media attention for something gimmicky got their reward: fifteen minutes of fame. And artists, performers, athletes, models, etc., were vetted through the appropriate channels. If a musical artist earned a Grammy® Award, they won the prize for a reason: genuine talent. Grammy® Awards were not handed out like candy to marginally talented people. The creative works of an artist had to be top-of-the-line. Back then, the competition was brutal because the talent on display was second to none, as the proverbial bar was set at the highest level – forcing artists to perfect their crafts and strive to bring forth their very best work.

What we see today would not have stood a chance then. Movies were (real) movies, motion pictures, not a damn video shot on an iPhone, and television sitcoms were the real deal, with professional performers portraying fictional characters written by industry-based teleplay writers, not everyday people (supposedly unscripted) on so-called reality shows.

Then, hard work was at the helm, not frivolity. Now, the bar is on the ground. Anybody can step over it.

There were always those fifteen-minute famous people in the past who made it their job to run in the same circles with legitimately famous people to obtain credibility. But it never lasted because, in the end, the legitimate always stood, and the illegitimate fell. Still, we see it today: those who claim to be "famous for being famous" rub shoulders with the legitimately famous in desperate pursuits of credibility – without talent.

Members of the general public (otherwise known as everyday people) on social media platforms with tons of "followers" and "likes" (organic or otherwise) do not constitute legitimate fame. Not unless they have contributed noted public works in professional industries, period.

Here lies the truth, but few are those who will embrace it. On the contrary, many have fallen head over heels in love with the illusion (and delusion) of a lie, like the young woman named Skye, who co-stars as the "Influencer" on the pages of the wicked (and downright sinister) psychological thriller currently under review.

Dear reader? Shall we get on with it – the (actual) review, that is?

There's No Time Like the Present...

- **THE CALM BEFORE THE STORM (I)**

Our leading man, Nathan Edwards, is a 44-year-old widower with two teenage daughters from his late wife, Sacha: Isla (15) and Chloe (13). The Edwards family lives in a splendid farmhouse in Sussex, a South East area of England. Nathan lost his first wife (and his first love), Sacha, to an advanced form of terminal cancer a few years back and is only recently learning to live and love again. And he's getting there, slowly but surely.

Nathan now shares his life with three ladies: his two daughters and Marie, his beautiful new fiancée. A 32-year-old former au pair turned lover and soon-to-be wife, Marie is everything to Nathan and his girls. She is not a replacement for Sacha; she is her own woman. And she is slowly settling into her new role within the family. The quiet but no-nonsense Marie respects not only herself but also Nathan and his history with Sacha. Not to mention, Marie, a native of Switzerland, is a fabulous cook. She is the perfect addition to the Edwards household.

Chloe loves Marie, but Isla? Isla—a girl out of whose mouth the taste I would slap if it were possible—is another animal. The disrespectful Isla dislikes Marie and continues to make her former au pair aware of her contempt in no uncertain terms. Isla has never moved on from the death of her beloved mum, Sacha, and she will not accept Marie as a stepmother. But Marie is patient. She loves Nathan and his girls, and there is nothing that she would not do for them. Nathan loves her, too. He loves Marie. They can make it – and they will.

What the happy couple is unaware of, however, is that there is a wicked storm on the horizon. And it is on course to make landfall over the peaceful dwelling of the Edwards family, to inflict chaos and uproot the tranquil foundation of their lives.

- **THE CALM BEFORE THE STORM (II)**

The plot begins to simmer as the Edwards clan is seated at their dinner table, enjoying a delicious Chicken Á L'Orange prepared by Marie. As far as Nathan is concerned, conversation keeps the family bond secure, and maintaining that closeness with his Gen Z daughters means the world to him. So, what better way to rope the girls in than to mention the hottest "stars" on Instagram, YouTube, and TikTok, particularly one named Skye, known for having millions of followers across the three major platforms?

Marie would like to know what the young woman is famous for, and she questions the two girls innocently. But Isla and Chloe, both dense as a rainforest, only roll their eyes at their out-of-touch stepmother-to-be and remind the old lady (even though Marie is only 32 years old) that Skye has millions of followers on YouTube, TikTok, and, duh, Insta. Still, the question remains: What is Skye famous for? Is she a singer? A writer? An actress? A filmmaker? What? Marie wants to know. But all her two impressionable (future) stepdaughters can answer is, 'You don't have to be good at something to be a social media celebrity. You only need to be authentic.' This idiotic answer elicits a smirk from Marie. And rightfully so. As Nathan puts it, hard work is the only thing that (really) matters. Recognition will follow if it's merited. But are Isla and Chloe soaking up any of that wisdom? No, the childish girls are not; their only interests are levels of popularity on social media platforms.

Skye, the social media darling, is looking to spread her "influential wings" by pursuing an ambassadorship with a charity of note. In this case, the formerly homeless Skye, who was raised in care because her drug-addicted mother chose to abandon her, has selected Sacha's Sanctuary, a charity for homeless individuals and families. Owned and managed by Nathan, Sacha's Sanctuary, named for the late Sacha Edwards, was initially founded by Nathan and Sacha as a successful catering business that earned them a handsome sum. But after Sacha's death, Nathan converted the entity to a charity for needy families.

Thus far, the charity has done well and is thriving on donations. But it could do much better. Old Scratch knows this and uses the opportunity to send an agent in the flesh to get the ball of mayhem rolling: a member of Skye's PR team. The person contacts Sacha's Sanctuary to inquire about the charity hiring Skye to front their fundraising campaign. And the starstruck staff at the Sanctuary are beside themselves with excitement. Nathan couldn't care less about her fame; he is not the social media-networking type. But if this influencer, Skye, wants to use her influence to help the charity with donations and growth, he is good with that. Sacha would be so proud of him and their charity.

Understandably, Nathan is not keen on telling the girls yet; they would never allow him a moment's rest due to their exhilaration. But he will have to, eventually, if his meeting with Skye's team at So She & All (*Social*, if one said the word quickly) goes well and Nathan decides to bring Skye on board.

- **THE CALM BEFORE THE STORM (III)**

The tall and awesomely beautiful Tiana Jackson is Skye's tenacious agent who is in for the long haul, literally and figuratively. She and her lucrative client, Skye—but especially her lucrative client, Skye—practically throw themselves at Nathan no sooner than he arrives for their meeting. Tiana is giddy and insists that Nathan partner up with Skye on behalf of Sacha's Sanctuary – to act as the charity's ambassador. No-nonsense, the model-like Tiana cuts right to the chase, doing all the talking as Skye sits, staring at the man she intends to make her own: Nathan Edwards.

While Tiana is going through her agent's pitch, Skye is already making love to Nathan—in the fantasy of her mind. She had greeted the handsome stranger with a kiss (although inappropriate) to test the boundaries. While air kissing the cheeks was the standard practice, Skye went for his lips. And if Nathan was put off by it, he didn't let on.
But then again, Nathan *is* a rather conservative, somewhat passive chap, bland as milquetoast (at times), and reserved to an annoying fault; this is why he won't be ready when the monster Category 5 hurricane—in the human form of a "famous social media influencer"—makes landfall, to beat,

with fists of fury, upon his quiet little house, to disrupt his quiet little life – with Marie and the girls.

The ill-prepared Nathan won't be ready.

Once Upon a Time...

- **AN OVERCAST ~~SKY~~ SKYE**

Before the so-called "Skye Effect" ever came into being, an English foster child, spawned from humble beginnings, lived in south-eastern London, where she spent most of her young life as a ward of the state – shuffled from one care home to another. But as she got older, the poor orphan became wiser, biding her time, keeping her head down, and eating whatever the low-quality fare was until she reached the age of seventeen; an opportunity to escape her hellish prison came then.

The criminals wanted to use her to sell their drugs, but she had other plans. She only needed a few dollars to get out; she only needed the sixty quid she stole from the dope pusher to kiss south-eastern London and her miserable existence in it goodbye, forever.

Whew! A train ride en route to an escape never felt so good.

The idyllic town of Horsham Centre would be the perfect place to straighten her nappy roots. Horsham Centre was discreet – and pretty. And it would be home. She was going to make it there; she had to. *She had to.*

Homeless and hungry, she used some of her stolen (drug) money to buy coffee and a bacon sandwich. And as she sat warming her bones in the cafe, she thought, deciding what to do next. She would need cardboard to sleep on—and a good storefront doorway to shield her from the elements.

Skye Walker (at least the trifling scourge who is her mother had a sense of humor) knew where she had been, but she couldn't begin to imagine where she would go.

- **INTRODUCING TIFFANY LARKIN**

Homeless and cold, Skye was sitting on the ground in a doorway, shaking her foot to keep the blood circulating, when she nearly tripped a strange young woman walking by. The girl, about the same age as the destitute Skye, seemed moved by compassion and empathy and offered Skye Walker fifty dollars. Skye took the money, of course, and could eat another day.

The first time, there were no formal introductions, but when the rich Tiffany Larkin saw Skye again, Tiffany offered her a trip to Starbucks for coffee and brownies. Skye accepted.

From that time on, the two young women became inseparable. Tiffany is a girl with everything except the love of her self-absorbed and browbeating, albeit filthy rich, parents, mom Adina (a beautiful former Czech model) and dad Jeffrey (an unattractive and obese master of horticulture and the so-called King of Salads). The statuesque Adina acts as though she is disgusted with her bosomy, somewhat plump daughter Tiffany – although she takes a liking to the more slender Skye almost immediately, cooking tasty meals and whatnot to win the skinny Minnie over.

After Tiffany convinces her mother that Skye is a friend from college, Adina invites the pauper to stay at Bashfield Manor, the nowhere-near-humble abode of the Larkins. Jeffrey, on the other hand, is not so okay with it. To live with them, Skye will have to pull her weight, the little her body has. And the mean-spirited—and arrogant—blob Jeffrey gets a brilliant idea: Skye will go to work at his salad factory. She can make some money, and everything will end well, right? Nothing could be more wrong, as the brutal labor and wrath-inducing humiliation Jeffrey Larkin subjects Skye to will set the man and his privileged family on a collision course with petrifying disaster.

- **SHE HAD BIG DREAMS, SHE WANTED FAME—
  WELL FAME COSTS**

Fame. That was what Tiffany Larkin coveted. She desired to be famous on YouTube but had no idea where to start. Tiffany wanted to do makeup tutorials that accumulated lots (and lots) of likes and lots (and lots) of followers. That was her only goal. She didn't give a damn about graduating from college with a degree in engineering and working in her dad's crappy salad-growing business (the same "crappy" salad-growing business that kept her living like a bloody princess); Tiffany only wanted the false honor of something called "Internet fame." The thing was, she sucked at it; even her fellow co-eds, the mean girls, took to YouTube to move their bowels on her posts. Tiffany was rich but pitiful. So Skye decided to help the poor little rich girl—with her unconfident, doughy ~~ass~~ arse—out.

Tiffany couldn't believe it when Skye posted a live video of herself sharing details about her plight with homelessness on Tiffany's YouTube channel. The post was "blessed" with so many likes that it made Tiffany's empty head spin.
Tiffany was a college student, but damn that; Tiffany was a pilot in training, learning to fly her family's private Cessna 182 alongside a licensed flying instructor, but damn that; Tiffany was a proficient sailor, but damn that, too. Skills couldn't hold a candle to social likes because the psychological aspect was as clear as spring water: social media post likes from strangers indicated a person was loved and perceived as valuable. And Tiffany honored *that* more.

Love was scarce in the Larkin home, as was self-love within Tiffany; therefore, Tiffany sought (external) love from strangers—on a social media platform.

But in the end, it was Skye who would shine. And resentments would display their displeasure. Before it was over, the same Cessna 182 owned by Jeffrey and Adina

Larkin, while speeding to one of their vacation homes in Jersey, would become their coffin at sea – deliberately brought down from its soaring heights into the English Channel.

Back to the Present – Ten Years Later...

- **UNDER A DARKENING ~~SKY~~ SKYE**

With foster homes, poverty, alienation, and obscurity behind her, Skye is now a 27-year-old rich and "mega-famous" social media influencer with brands, agents, and everyone else, for that matter, eating out of her baby-soft hands. Everyone except Nathan Edwards, that is. And that is not good because Skye has her sights set on him, and she is opposed to being rejected, least of all by the only man who has ever hushed her puppies. Sure, she claims to be dating a world-famous athlete, a champion sailor named Holden, but that so-called relationship is as shallow as a reef wall and only for the public; there are no true feelings there.

Skye wants Nathan; he is all she can think about – and at present, she's watching the nervous wreck fidget. *God, why can't he relax?!*

Nathan feels awkward and out of place at the fancy granola brand event. Skye knows it, so she uses the situation to her advantage. Emotionally weak men like Nathan are almost always easy to manipulate. And all Skye had to do was keep feeding him liquor, not forgetting to spike one glass. With that, a naked Nathan would awaken the following morning in her bed with no memory whatsoever of what happened the night before. He knows Marie will be furious that he stayed out all night without even so much as one phone call – but his phone was off. And Nathan *never* turns his phone off. At this point, his suspicions towards Skye are beginning to heat up.

His entire team at Sacha's Sanctuary, including his number-one wingman, the big-and-bearish Ash, is elated that they captured Skye to serve as an ambassador for the charity. And they're gushing, all teeth and rosy cheeks. But at what price? Not one of them could imagine the dynamic between the desperate and obsessed Skye—who has, by now, chased the jealous and confused Marie away and won the hearts of Isla and Chloe—and Nathan, who dares to spurn the relentless advances of the ridiculously popular influencer. But Nathan Edwards better recognize. Skye always gets what she wants – or else. Unfortunately for Skye, she's not the only one with lustful ambition.

- **THAT'S MY MAMA**

Skye is so carried away in her infatuation with the man named Nathan Edwards that she doesn't see the hit coming. Indeed, it is true what they say about folks suddenly coming out of the woodwork when someone they know comes into fame and money. And for Skye, the adage becomes only too real when the woman reaches out to her on Facebook. Skye ignores her, but then the woman shows up, unannounced, at her opulent home – an old, skinny, wrinkled, wretched, and disgusting body of flesh, given a yuck mouth with which to speak.

Her name is Monica Walker, and she is Skye's long-lost and long-thought-to-be-dead mother. She claims that she has been clean and sober for years, but the ravages of a life once lived in the Taj Mahal of dope fiends are irreparable. Monica seems to mean well, as she is frantic for a chance to right the wrongs of the past and reconcile with her only daughter, Skye. But Skye *hates* the woman and wants nothing more than for the old bag to disappear and not stay around to complicate her fabulous new life in the public eye. Monica abandoned Skye, and Skye will never allow her to forget it. But Monica? Monica is adamant. The woman is also skeptical – a little too dubious for Skye's liking. And she is making Skye nervous. Indeed, the tension between the two is so thick that one could cut it with a hacksaw.

To show good faith, as well as for her public image, Skye agrees to "reconcile" with Monica publicly, but she soon gets too cute, pulling a loose string to unravel that which should have remained tightly knitted. Now Monica wants a pound of flesh, making threats while asking for more than Skye is willing to give. But Monica is about to dip her crusty, corny toes in a vat of acid - as she is so determined to expose a most damning secret about her daughter that *she* won't see the hit coming.

It only gets worse for Monica after she meets Nathan.

As far as Skye is concerned, this peasant, Monica, will have to go before she ruins *EVERYTHING* Skye has worked so hard for! Skye cannot afford to have this—this ignoramus interfering in her life, trying to destroy her beloved brand and her pristine public image. No, this heinous freak has to go – for good!

With her immoral mind finally made up, Skye pulls out her trusty burner phone and makes a fateful call.

- **I ~~CAN'T~~ WILL MAKE YOU LOVE ME (EVEN) IF YOU DON'T**

Skye is tired of chasing Nathan like a thirsty idiot – only to have him consistently rebuff her shameless advances. After all, she has her (silly) pride to defend. And *that*, she will.

When he got his bloody frickin' noggin cracked, Skye catered to his every whim following the murky attack, even bringing him floral bouquets. But what did the ungrateful bloke do? He *whined* for *Marie*. When she exposed her sheer nudity to him, what did he do? He *groaned* for *Marie*. ~~Marsha~~ Marie, ~~Marsha~~ Marie, ~~Marsha~~ Marie!

The former nanny (a frickin' *nobody*) undoubtedly overshadows Skye (the social media star), and Skye's frail ego can't handle it.

Nathan has no intention of leaving Marie for Skye, nor will he ever bend the knee of affection to her. The man cannot make his heart feel something it won't. And for this reason, she, Skye, must now unleash the barbaric bitch – who is always ready, willing, and able to spill blood.

If expensive dinners and expensive gifts and intimate gestures or the sword she is holding over his head won't win Nathan over, perhaps losing yet another of his precious loved ones (to homicide) will.

Here is where Nathan Edwards will become "Dan Gallagher," and Skye, the social media influencer, will become "Alex Forrest."
Skye will *NOT* take no for an answer. She will *NOT* be ignored—by the object of her twisted desires. Nathan *will* be hers because if she, the famous Skye with her unfailing "Skye Effect," can't have him, *NO OTHER PERSON*, not even his two spoiled, bratty, fanatical daughters, will!

Five people will be dead, insensitively murdered, before Nathan Edwards understands that.

Meeting the Bit Players...

In addition to the tall, dark, and ultra-lovely Tiana Jackson, who plays her part to perfection as Skye's ambitious agent on these pages, a few more bit players also carry their weight flawlessly and finely complement our starring leads. Meet them as follows:

- Pete Brandine is like family to Nathan, a dear old friend who glorifies Skye and urges Nathan to welcome her as the figurehead ambassador for Sacha's Sanctuary. But like all the others, Pete only sees the deceptive surface.

- Ellie, another dear friend of the Edwards family, is a godsend in the absence of Marie.

- Martin Rodriguez is a low-down, dirty, crooked, lying, fork-tongued celebrity journalist at the *Daily Mail.* He smiles a crap-eating grin—revealing sharpened teeth—while keeping a dagger handy for the backstab: it was Martin Rodriguez who sold Skye out, dishing the details of her whereabouts to Monica, all in the name of a story guaranteed to rake in the big bucks.

- Camilla Steading plays a relocation agent (or a real estate "specialist," if you will) to the rich, famous, and high-profile. Camilla is a fast talker, a wheeler, and a dealer—but Skye is worse. Unbeknownst to Camilla, she is about to be used as a tool to carry out the twisted wishes of the evil one.

- Detective Constable Dominic McCarthy is the instant karma who will get medieval if it's the last thing he does: woe unto the fandom.

My Summation...

Narrated in the multiple viewpoints of Nathan, Skye, and Isla, *The Influencer* is a terrifying foray into the desperate pursuit of fame, riches, and love that eludes.
On the rapid-fire pages of this skillfully written tale, Miranda Rijks unlocks a forbidden door that leads to a very dark place in the human mind – a place laid waste to distortion, deceit, madness, wickedness, aberrance, perversion, corruption, and everything debased. Here, Miranda Rijks takes a sledgehammer to the layered falsities of social media, smashing them away to uncover the truth.
Indeed, the author's writing is sensational, as is her knowledge of several topics that rouse my (personal) interest, including sailing and Regatta. With *The Influencer*, Rijks was on it, and she blew me away.

The concept here is nothing less than entertaining, and Miranda Rijks maneuvered her vision expertly to showcase a great plot, a great cast of characters, nearly blemish-free character development, and applaudable performances. And I am impressed.

The story on the pages of *The Influencer* is a cautionary tale of social media and its crippling influence on unstable individuals on whom worldliness, pride, ego, self-hatred, low self-esteem, confusion, envy, jealousy, false idolatry, emotional dependency, neediness, depression, anxiety, hatred, malice, and all other (demonic) forms of wickedness prey.

An empty soul seeking external validation will never be satisfied. People must first love themselves before they can love anyone else. And they must know who they are rather than waiting for someone else to tell them who they are. All other roads only lead one down the path of destruction. Faith—is a wonderful thing. But on the pages of this sadistic narrative, many characters are faithless and not at all what (or who) they appear to be.

Speaking now of Miranda Rijks, after reading the blurbs of all her books and sensing that each title would be individually intriguing, I settled on *The Influencer* first. And I am so glad I did because, from beginning to end, it is an outstanding psychological thriller loaded with one crazy twist after another, leading the way to a heart-pounding cliffhanger of a conclusion.

Dear reader, while I prepare to absorb my second Miranda Rijks tale, *The Homemaker*, I leave you with my highest recommendation of *The Influencer*, as I am sure you will find it as hard to put down as I did.
Enjoy!

Five...marketed-and-endorsed stars.

DISCLOSURE: The reference to the fictional characters "Dan Gallagher" and "Alex Forrest" is from the Adrian Lyne-directed and Paramount Pictures-distributed thriller film "Fatal Attraction" (1987)

Acknowledgments

First and foremost, I praise my Father God, my Lord, Christ Jesus, and His glorious Holy Spirit for their mercy, love, and great blessings.

I glorify my Lord for the gifts He has implanted in me because I would amount to nothing minus Him. Once again, my Heavenly Father has used me to produce His work according to His divine will. And I did so with faith, wisdom, patience, and humility as my guiding forces. Thank You, Lord God, for bestowing upon me honor as Your servant and completing this new creative work that, without Your blessing, would never have come into being. I love You with everything I have in me.

Joe, Nathaniel, Nairobi, Naras, Maurice, and Freddie, thank you, my nearest and dearest, for supporting me on my journey when many others did not. I will NEVER forget how much you all cared for me and encouraged me. True friendship and love don't cost a thing. And I love all of you—unconditionally.

Thank you to my phenomenal team at Quill Pen Ink Publishing. Nicky, Big Timmy Mac, Char, Benji (Welcome to the QPIP family, Benj!), Terri, and Twix, you all deserve raises! You are all members of my extended family, and I love you just the same. I adore all of you, and I thank you for going that extra mile with me. Let's keep going.

Thank you to my readers, who will always have a special place in my heart. I write for the love of writing and do so with the anticipation of you all viewing the body texts of my words. My dear readers, it means everything that each of you finds my creative writing fun and fascinating. I've learned a lot throughout my life thus far, and it is pleasing to share wisdom, knowledge, and understanding not only about life but also the nature of people through my compositions. Thank you, my dear readers, for sticking with me on this writing journey, as you are all the cherished ones I love to create for. There's still more to come, so stay tuned.

All my love,

Cat Ellington

Coming Soon

The Arts of Literary Criticism:
Romance in Haiku, Book 2
Cover Hue: Lilac Shimmer

About the Author

Cat Ellington is an American songwriter/composer, casting director, poet, author, voice-over actress, and entrepreneur from Chicago, IL. She is best known for her prolific contributions to the music industry, the motion picture industry, and literature.

Cat Ellington's professional credits list a library of nonfiction books, including the Reviews by Cat Ellington series, *The Making of Dual Mania*, *More Imaginative Than Ordinary Speech*, *Memoirs in Gogyohka*, and *You Can Quote Me On That*. In film and music, Ellington's credentials include her work on the psychological thriller, "Dual Mania," and its soundtrack—on which she wrote five original songs: "The

Book of Us," "I'm Still in Love," "Something in Your Eyes," "Gett Out, and "I Do."

Outside of her professional element, the award-winning creative enjoys reading, listening to music, cooking, collecting vintage and modern charm bracelets, watching movies and classic TV shows, sailing, jet-skiing, playing tennis, and eating frozen yogurt – lots of it.

[Cat Ellington on Amazon: Books, Biography, Blog, Audiobooks, Kindle](#)

[Cat Ellington at the Award-Winning Boutique Domain](#)

[Cat Ellington at the Review Period with Cat Ellington](#)

[Cat Ellington at IMDb](#)

"Romance in Haiku"

A Prelude to *The Arts of Literary Criticism: Romance in Haiku, Book 2*

poetic hearts beat—
to a haiku for lovebirds:
beaks rubbed in euphoric bliss

www.ingramcontent.com/pod-product-compliance
Lightning Source LLC
Chambersburg PA
CBHW060506090426
42735CB00011B/2124